100 Questions and Answers: Religion in America

100 Questions and Answers:

Religion in America

By George Gallup, Jr.

and

Sarah Jones

Princeton Religion Research Center

1989

ISBN 0-940303-01-9

Book design by Donald Fox,
Wayman Williams and
Michael Helmstadter.
Cover design by Leslie Mullen.

Printed by Hermitage Press.

Library of Congress Catalog Card Number: 89-61701

Table of Contents

VII. **Spiritual Development and Commitment**

VIII. **Trends**

X. **Methodology**

Preface

Most Americans believe in God, in miracles, eternal judgment and moral absolutes. But fewer are joining churches and synagogues. Public opinion of organized religion is changing, even though huge majorities still cling to basic teachings of the biblical tradition. Religious faith in this country today may be more a private matter than shared experience.

Based on a range of questions put to the U.S. public, this book takes a hard look at religion in America from the ground up. *100 Questions and Answers* responds to the many inquiries that come to our offices in Princeton, New Jersey from members of the media, the academic community, from clergy, lay religious leaders and other segments of the population. We arranged the questions by categories: personal beliefs and practices, church and synagogue, organized religion and society, religious experience and spiritual development.

Nearly all the surveys are based on samples of adults eighteen and older, and some on samples of teens. Many samples were regretably too small to include Jews, Eastern and Russian Orthodox, and other religious groups in the analyses. A glossary appears at the end of the book to clarify our terms and to assist students of religion.

We would like to thank Kenneth Briggs, Jim Castelli, Elizabeth Gilliam, Miriam Murphy and John F. Wilson for their many helpful suggestions.

George Gallup, Jr.
Sarah Jones

Princeton, New Jersey

Introduction

Liberty is the founding premise of religion in America, more religiously committed than any nation in the Western world. Since 1791 the Bill of Rights has guaranteed public and private exercise of religious freedom, which ended centuries of trials for heresy as treason. Here the rule of tolerance gave rise to a deeply pluralistic, voluntary republic whose early settlers based their vision of social unity on religious coherence. Perhaps this country's most coherent but diverse expression of unity is belief in God — cited in the Declaration of Independence and today by more than nine in ten adults nationwide.

Sociologist Daniel Bell argues that beliefs are independent of changes in the social structure, a thesis supported by the stability of Gallup trends on religious beliefs. In fifty years the nation's social order has undergone rapid and profound transformations with little effect on measures of personal faith. The character of public faith has changed dramatically, however, and the religious free market competing for members has become so fragmented that any one description is partial at best. The following hundred questions trace very real but disparate elements of the religious climate, questions presupposing a past that shaped key indicators of America's spiritual mood. What does the past tell us about the present?

If there were one true story of religion in America, it would begin with immigrants seeking religious and economic freedoms — radical Puritans in the Northeast sure of providential favor, and enterprising Anglicans in the South — soon joined by Baptists, Quakers, Methodists, Presbyterians, Lutherans, Catholics, Jews and more. By the time Thomas Jefferson declared a "wall of separation" between church and state, most of today's major denominations were in place. Still, a vast unchurched majority held until the Great Awakenings, when Methodist and Baptist revivals made these the country's largest denominations and secured an evangelical ethos within the Protestant mainstream. Even more remarkable was the growth resulting from the legal separation of church and state, an action upheld by religious and political leaders alike.

Expanding religious communities of the nineteenth century gave millions of new immigrants a home for voluntary worship independent of pressures to assimilate. After the Civil War, with urbanization and the rise of a new industrial and class economy, those pressures mounted nonetheless. Feelings of religious ethnicity would gradually give way to patriotic piety as America rose to a world power, whose

Protestant majority segregated by race and class had once thought capital gain a sign of virtue. Largely because of the Protestant ethic, individualism took root in the national psyche with irreversible effects on organized religion and public morality.

At the turn of the century patterns of affiliation began to reflect the emerging modern temperament given to experiment, mobility and economic progress. Fewer Americans joined churches for reasons of ascription or kinship, and more out of personal choice: what Max Weber called elective affinity had figured widely in the impact of unprecedented movements and charismatic leaders such as Mary Baker Eddy and Christian Science, Joseph Smith and Mormonism, and Ellen White and Seventh Day Adventism. Ongoing waves of immigration and relocations from farms to cities pluralized the more traditional base of Catholics, Protestants and Jews, which to some extent divided these groups into subcultures across regions. The process anticipated later developments among religious conservatives and liberals, each with unique demographies and conflicting rules for interpreting scriptures and ethical life.

Those conflicts erupted in a Tennessee courtroom in 1925 when John Scopes faced criminal charges for teaching evolution to high school students. Never before had the lines been drawn so sharply between fundamentalists and modernists, and the reverberations were felt throughout the country in churches, colleges and legislatures. The prominence of liberal theology prior to World War I now came under fire from growing ranks of fundamentalists opposed to preaching historical exegesis and the ambiguities of good and evil.

The controversy galvanized evangelical churches, but less conservative mainline membership declined amid strife that drove many to communities outside churches and synagogues. Purpose groups sprang up for voluntary service and reform of voting and labor laws, public health and education; issues earlier brought to focus by such movements as the Social Gospel and women's rights. Also, far from Scopes's rural South, technology and the artistic renaissance of the 1920s introduced middle class urban Americans to affordable leisure, with permanent secularizing effects on the culture and religious bodies. Apart from the roaring new prosperity of the jazz age, social scientists spoke of alienation and Freud of religious neurosis, a topic under wide discussion which distanced many thinking people from organized religion in the U.S.

The crash of 1929 ended the decade with an American tragedy that forced churches and synagogues to adjust to national poverty and massive dislocations of the population. Clergy and theologians struggled to give meaning to the experience as Americans mobilized under Roosevelt's New Deal, vigorously supported by Episcopalian and Jewish leadership. Critiques of capitalism came from Methodist and Presbyterian church officials, and praise from the Southern Baptist Convention. Roughly seven in ten U. S. adults claimed church membership during the Depression years, which fostered a needed spirit of religious and national unity despite persisting ideological and doctrinal differences among conservatives and liberals. Beyond the help of the public support programs, those hardest hit banded together among themselves: rural Americans, blacks, ethnic groups. Fundamentalist churches doubled in size. Mainstream membership dwindled. Religious pluralism would remain a fact of the culture, but the common plight of Americans drew the less stricken to interdenominational efforts still prevalent today.

One of the most influential was Neo-orthodoxy, a theological reform movement inspired by Reinhold and H. Richard Niebuhr and chiefly developed by Karl Barth in Europe during the Second World War. Critical of liberal idealism, Neo-orthodoxy nevertheless offered a message of hope and statements on social justice much in keeping with the tenor of the New Deal. Realistic, evangelical and humanistic, it recognized doctrinal diversity and so found its way into Roman Catholic and mainline Protestant communities alike. The movement stressed biblical authority and the basic Christian message of grace, redemption and atonement, a teaching all churchgoers could hear. Neo-orthodoxy reconciled religious conservatives and liberals. From the work of H. Richard Niebuhr it also explained demographic divisions within denominations, just before Gallup first conducted religion polls in the mid-1930s.

Neo-orthodox theologians would join the resistance against Hitler in Germany, while in the U.S. the bombing of Pearl Harbor in 1941 signaled the end of the Great Depression. The war economy would make the nation the world's strongest political and economic power, removed from threats to civilian populations in Europe. Americans now fully employed entered the age of technology conscious of a national and religious identity, but a moral consensus was lacking in churches, still polarized and less of a presence than during the First World War in shaping public values. Religious affiliation stepped up somewhat; voluntary service agencies and home mission programs multiplied. A Gallup survey in 1942 showed four in ten U.S. clergy opposed to or unsure about organized religious support of the war effort, suggesting the influence of pacifist activity launched among clergy after World War I.

The years following World War II ushered in the postwar revival of religious life in the U.S., in large measure a celebration of patriotic national values. Church attendance reached high points in 1955 and 1958 during a time most indicators of religious impact climbed to record highs as well. Much of the membership, at the peak of 76% in 1947 and on the whole younger than today, migrated to burgeoning suburbs where millions of veterans began families. With the help of new religious media and Eisenhower's compelling rhetoric of God and country, many Americans linked the conservative cause of freedom with religious faith and anticommunism. These were the years Joseph McCarthy mounted the so-called Red Scare against "moral anarchy" and dissenting advocates of freedom of speech and expression. A 1954 Gallup Poll reported 46% of the U.S. public with a "favorable opinion" of McCarthy.

A year later Will Herberg published a landmark study of America's triple melting pot in *Protestant–Catholic–Jew*, citing a Gallup survey that showed 53% of the population unable to name any of the four Gospels. Herberg claimed the postwar revival lacked the substance of the major faiths, even though it gave people a sense of identity and belonging in pluralistic culture. Being Protestant, Catholic or Jewish meant being American and sharing in the American Dream, a secular symbol of prosperity and power with tacit implications for blacks and women.

In the 1960s Baptist minister Martin Luther King, Jr. voiced his own dream of equal opportunity, supported in 1988 by nine in ten Americans (91%). The civil rights movement brought evangelical minority ethics before the nation in an effort that would redefine the legal scope of pluralism in the U.S. At the same time women organized across the country to redress inequalities of public and private values in America, one lasting result being the ordination of women in mainline Protestant churches and Reform synagogues. Theologies of liberation came from women and blacks during the 1960s, when the civil religious morality of the previous decade began to dissolve in waves of protest against the Viet Nam War; when situation ethicists called love the only viable code of moral action free of absolutes unsuited to given conditions. American institutions became a source of disillusion. The moral and spiritual authority of the religious mainstream seemed to be eroding.

Since then traditional preference groups have gradually altered their organized ties, and the coupling of religious and national identities has taken more individual and diverse forms of religious expression. Americans giving no religious preference has risen from 2% in 1952 to 10% in 1988. The nation's unchurched population at 44% has grown slightly over the past decade.

The Protestant majority has steadily declined from 67% in 1952 to 56% in 1988, with notable drops in membership in the historic liberal mainline since the 1960s. Disproportionately represented by persons over fifty, the Protestant Episcopal Church and the Presbyterian Church (U.S.A.) have each lost over a million members since 1960; the United Church of Christ, about a half million. Membership has declined as well among moderate mainstream communities such as the United Methodist Church and the Evangelical Lutheran Churches of America, also aging denominations. But the conservative Southern Baptist Convention has grown and remains the nation's largest Protestant denomination, with 14.5 million members representing Christianity's strongest evangelical communion. Six in ten Southern Baptists called themselves born-again Christians, a proportion double that of all Americans. Importantly, 78% of African Americans give a Protestant preference, mostly Baptist and Methodist, powerfully represented in the contemporary evangelical tradition. Taken together the Protestant population is a vast and diffuse grouping with a staggering diversity of religious practices, moralities and systems of meaning surrounding the word and spirit of scriptures. To speak of a unified or national Protestant identity is no longer possible.

To some extent the same is true for American Catholics. Twenty-eight percent of the U.S. public call themselves Catholic, up almost half in the past forty years of increasing birth rates and an influx of Catholic Hispanic immigrants. For generations Catholics held to their ethnic roots in blue-collar families loyal to the Democratic Party and heavily concentrated in the industrialized East and Midwest. In 1986, although 41% of Catholics still lived in the East, the Sunbelt claimed 34%, many of whom were new immigrants from Mexico, Cuba, Southern Asia and Haiti. For the first time in the nation's history Catholics have become as prosperous as Protestants, in a dramatic shift Joseph Berger has called the demographics of affluence among educated Catholics now sweeping the professions and positions of leadership in big business and public policy. The Catholic Church has been the nation's largest denomination since the nineteenth century, with an estimated 52 million adherents — many increasingly skeptical of Vatican teachings on sexual ethics and the role of women in the public realm.

American Jews, broadly liberal politically and socially, have comprised 2% of the adult population since the early 1970s, a figure that fell steadily from 5% in 1947 to 3% during the 1950s and 1960s. Heavily concentrated in the East (58%), Jews in this country are re-evaluating Jewish identity and unity in a time of assimilation and the resulting trend toward secularization. Identified in varying degrees with a religion, an ethnicity and the Israeli nationality, fewer U.S. Jews are participating in Orthodox circles than in less traditional movements among Conservative and Reform communities. Each shares with the Orthodox a religious life based on interpretations of the Torah. Moreover, the gradual "Americanization" of the nation's Jewry has created a climate of disaffiliation signaled by the growing rate of intermarriage and a lower birth rate. In addition the current upheaval in Gaza and on the West Bank has raised questions of identity with Israel and has splintered the American Jewish community, historically united to defend Israel.

The percentage of Jews in the U.S. currently matches the proportion of Mormons or Latter-day Saints (2%), which reveals the shifts that have taken place in the tripartite religious culture Herberg described. Mormons are more fervent, more rapidly growing and more identified with one region that any of the nation's major denominations but Southern Baptists. Of about four million adherents nationwide, 77% live in the West and 57% in the Rocky Mountain states, their stronghold since Brigham Young, a converted Methodist, led them there from Missouri to the Salt Lake basin in 1847. During the past four decades they have grown over fivefold, due largely to a high birth rate and systematic evangelization. Mormon confessions and creeds developed apart from Protestant and Catholic theologies, although Latter-day Saints now represent 1% of the country's evangelical or born-again Christians, a designation shared by 20% of all Mormons.

With the possible exception of Mormons, the major religious groups in America reflect internal divisions of the culture between liberals and conservatives; divisions that trace less to ascriptive ties than personal determinations of morality and life style. Since the early 1970s the steady advance of the evangelical movement toward the religious mainstream has polarized many mainline constituencies. The most conservative of these have broken off and formed countless independent splinter churches that blur denominational boundaries and reinforce the transdenominational character of American evangelicalism.

During the past decade the evangelical movement has claimed more than a third of the U.S. public (33%). In recent years, however, organized religion as a whole has lost members, influence and public confidence, down seven percentage points between 1985 and 1988. Church and synagogue membership dipped to its lowest level ever recorded by Gallup in 1988, when eight in ten Americans said that religious beliefs should be decided independently of organized religion. Half of the population reported a decreasing religious impact, and just over a third cited an increase — a reversal of the trend recorded in 1986. Only 4% described faith in terms of religious affiliation. Attendance in 1988 was stable, but better than seven in ten agreed that a person can be "a good Christian or Jew" without attending church or synagogue.

Why the disaffection? Nearly all Americans believe in God, and 84% in the divinity of Christ, up from 78% in 1978 — an increase found also among the unchurched, 71% of whom believe Jesus is God or the Son of God — suggesting a trend toward dislocation of private faith from organized religion. In the year that church and synagogue membership fell to a historic low, over half nationwide said religion is "very important" in their personal lives, while most cited beliefs and practices common to traditional organized religious teachings. Eight in ten agreed the Bible is the word of God, and overwhelming majorities said they believe in miracles, the last judgment and life after death. Seventy-six percent agreed "completely" or "mostly" that prayer is an important part of everyday life. Roughly six in ten of those without a religious preference said they never doubt the existence of God.

These findings indicate the extent of traditional spirituality in the private lives of Americans, but others point to public dissatisfaction with clergy and the general direction of organized religion. In 1985 67% of Americans gave the clergy "high" or "very high" ratings of their ethical standards. In 1988 the figure fell to 60%. Related surveys showed that Americans have become more critical of their churches in the past decade. A large majority felt that churches give undue emphasis to internal organizational issues and not enough to spirituality. A plurality reported the churches are not enough concerned about social justice.

Other factors figure in the trends toward religious privacy and away from organized commitment. Denominational switching has increased since the 1960s, a reflection of the wider range of options for Americans to choose among religious and quasi-religious communities. According to a recent Gallup study fewer than half of U.S. adults (43%) say they have always been a member of their present denomination. Also, small purpose groups have grown faster than churches and synagogues; especially Bible studies, which have drawn some 46 million nationwide to a base of intimacy many large churches cannot provide. More generally, the conservative-liberal split has divided the moral concensus of the religious mainstream, at a time when Americans are seeking a cogent moral foundation for themselves and their children — something seen to be lacking among a few of the most visible TV evangelists in the U.S.

The resurgence of traditional family values in America finds ample support in Gallup measures of the ethical priorities among adults. In 1988 nearly all (94%) said they would welcome stronger family ties. In 1989 nine in ten (89%) assigned the top position on an eleven-point scale to the importance of having a good family life. The figures underscore an ideal denied by a soaring divorce rate and actual breakdown of the nuclear family in America.

Much has been said about moral pluralism in connection with the social experiments of the 1960s. On the eve of the 1990s, however, eight in ten nationwide agree "completely" or "mostly" that absolute standards of good and evil apply universally. The eclipse of situation ethics in America appears to be underway, although expressions of individual and private morality are evolving in isolation from religious communities once said to be the nation's ethical conscience. Americans have relinquished the patriotic piety of the 1950s, but continue on a private search for personal and moral meaning less tied to organized bodies with conflicting or equivocal rules of conduct. According to a recent Gallup survey, seven in ten U.S. adults say the conviction that life has meaning or purpose is "very important." By rule of law people are free to seek meaning in unorthodoxy, in the New Age movement, for example. The voluntary religious tradition in this country reflects the cultural climate at large. Still, for most Americans, belief in God endures the effects of change.

100 Questions and Answers: Religion in America

I. Religious Beliefs

Alexis de Toqueville called America a nation of believers, as true now as in 1831 when he toured the country and came to know its democratic "soul of a church." Today nearly all U.S. adults (94%) say they believe in God or a universal spirit, a steady finding since the advent of scientific polling in the mid-1930s, and an indication of the stability of Americans' basic religious beliefs.

The gap between believing and belonging is widening, however, with church and synagogue membership down and a slight but steady increase in the unchurched population, while the growing percentage who believe in the divinity of Christ has risen six percentage points between 1978 and 1988. The differences are modest but meaningful because levels of belief and commitment change slowly in the Gallup trend surveys. These and related findings signal a climate of religious privacy, in the tradition shared among many of the nation's founders, most of whom nonetheless attended church.

Current patterns of privatization may undermine communal faith, but most Americans still adhere to key church doctrines: 84% believe Jesus Christ is God or the Son of God, and nearly as many, 80%, believe in the last judgment. In 1982 six in ten (62%) harbored "no doubts" about the Second Coming. An astounding eight in ten Americans (80%) express some measure of belief in miracles.

Within this traditional framework, recent surveys point to a widespread diversity of beliefs about images of God. Most Americans in 1984 were likely to name traditional images such as Father, Master, Judge and Redeemer, although significant minorities saw God as Mother, Healer and Liberator.

In addition 71% in 1988 said they believe in life after death, virtually the same proportion recorded over the past twenty yers. The same percentage (71%) in 1981 reported belief in heaven and eternal reward. Far fewer (53%) believe in a literal hell and only 20% deny the Devil exists as a person or an entity.

These and similar beliefs came under scrutiny during the late nineteenth century, when many intellectuals predicted the erosion of traditional Christianity by scientific inquiries into evolution and the historical accuracy of the Bible. If the survey data serve as a guide, such predictions never materialized in America.

According to a 1988 survey on beliefs about the Bible, for example, a combined total of 77% agreed the Bible is the actual or inspired word of God, with 55% subscribing to inerrancy and 22% admitting historical and scientific fallacies. The total percentage recorded in 1988 has increased moderately since 1985 (72%), during the same time the number believing literally in the Bible has dropped slightly from 34% in 1985 to 31% in 1988. Moreover, the proportion of fundamentalists — Americans who think the Bible is literally true — fell dramatically between 1963 (65%) and 1978 (37%).

Well over a century after Darwin published his theories of evolution in *The Origin of the Species*, a striking 44% believe in creationism: that living things came into being suddenly at some time within the last 10,000 years as a result of an act of God. A 38% minority believes in evolution with God and 9% in evolution without God, while another 9% are uncertain.

Many Americans, on the other hand, have taken up ideas often linked with the New Age movement. Twenty-three percent in 1981 subscribed to reincarnation, a belief more popular among the unchurched (27%), but evident among regular churchgoers as well (17%). The number of adults congenial to astrology dropped sharply over the last decade, from 29% in 1978 to 12% in 1988, compared to a 58% majority of teens cited in 1988. In 1987 half the adult population (50%) agreed that extraterrestrial life exists, up from 46% in 1973 and 34% in 1966 — perhaps due to relevant speculations in the scientific community.

Orthodox or not, most Americans seek meaningful lives. According to a 1985 survey, for seven in ten (70%) the belief that "life is meaningful or has a purpose" is "very important" — even if their search for meaning remains largely a private matter.

VAST MAJORITY BELIEVE IN GOD

Question:
Do you believe in God or a universal spirit?

	Yes %	No %	No Opinion %
NATIONAL	94	5	1
Men	90	7	3
Women	97	3	*
Whites	93	5	2
Blacks	99	1	*
Protestants	98	2	*
Catholics	96	1	3
Born-again Christians	100	*	*

*Less than one percent.

Beliefs About God

Heavenly father who can be reached by prayers	84 %
Idea, not a being	5
Impersonal Creator	2
Don't know	4
Do not believe in God or a universal spirit	5
	100 %

Findings are based on telephone interviews with 1,013 adults nationwide during February 1986.

Source: Gallup Survey for the Christian Broadcasting Network, Inc.

An overwhelming majority of American adults, 94%, believe in God or a universal spirit. A lesser but vast proportion, 84% , believe in a personal God who can be reached by prayers, while 5% understand God abstractly as an idea, and 2% say God is an impersonal creator. Five percent say they don't believe in God.

By most measures more spiritually active, women are more likely than men to believe in God by 97% to 90%. Levels of belief in God rise with age, while the college educated are somewhat less likely to believe than persons with less formal education. Belief in God is most prominent in the South, among lower income groups and among blacks.

The proportional difference between Protestants and Catholics is slight at 98% to 93%. Evangelical or born-again Christians believe unanimously at 100%.

DIVINITY OF CHRIST AFFIRMED BY 84%

Question:

What do you believe about Jesus Christ—do you think Jesus Christ was God or Son of God, another religious leader like Mohammed or Buddha, or do you think Jesus Christ never lived?

	God or Son of God %	Another Leader %	Never Actually Lived %	Other %	No Opinion %
NATIONAL	84	9	1	2	4
Men	79	11	1	3	6
Women	88	7	1	1	3
18-24 years	86	6	1	1	6
25-29 years	82	11	1	3	3
30-49 years	83	10	1	2	4
50 and older	85	8	1	1	5
Whites	82	10	1	2	5
Blacks	94	2	1	1	2
Hispanics	89	6	*	1	4
Protestants	92	4	*	1	3
Catholics	91	6	*	*	3
Other	35	40	4	10	11

*Less than one percent.

		1988			1978	
Belief	**Total %**	**Churched %**	**Unchurched %**	**Total %**	**Churched %**	**Unchurched %**
God or Son of God	84	93	71	78	89	64
Another Leader	9	4	15	13	6	21
Never Actually Lived	1	*	2	1	*	2
Other	2	1	4	2	1	3
No Opinion	4	2	8	6	4	10

*Less than one percent.

Findings are based on personal interviews with 2,556 adults nationwide during March 1988.

Source: Gallup Survey for the National Catholic Evangelization Association

The question of Christ's deity concerns a key component of orthodox Christianity expressed in creeds affirming God was incarnate in Christ, a biblical precept systematized during the fourth century at the Nicene church councils. It also concerns an experience or inner conviction of the divinity of Christ — which 84% of Americans affirm — considerably more than the proportion recorded in 1978 (78%).

The ten-year trend shows increases among the churched and unchurched as well. Ninety-three percent of churchgoers affirmed the incarnation in 1988, and 89% in 1978. A striking 72% of unchurched Americans believe in Christ's divinity, up from 64% ten years ago.

Only 9% feel that Jesus was "a religious leader like Mohammed or Buddha," fewer than the 13% in 1978. One percent say he "never actually lived," the same percentage cited in the previous survey.

Although current levels of belief are fairly constant among all population groups, blacks (94%) are more likely than whites (82%) and Hispanics (89%) to say Jesus was divine. Vast majorities of Protestants (92%) and Catholics (91%) affirm this belief, with those of other faiths more evenly divided between beliefs in the deity of Christ (35%) and his role as another religious leader (40%).

In terms of gender, women are more likely than men to view Jesus as God or Son of God by 88% to 79%. By age, persons between 18 and 24 (86%) and over 50 (85%) say Jesus was divine more frequently than those 25 to 29 (82%) and 30 to 49 (83%).

INTERPRETATIONS OF THE BIBLE VARY

Question:
Which of the statements on this card comes closest to describing your feelings about the Bible?

The Bible is the actual word of God and is to be taken literally, word for word.
The Bible is the inspired word of God. It contains no errors, but some verses are to be taken symbolically rather than literally.
The Bible is the inspired word of God, but it may contain historical and scientific errors.
The Bible was not inspired by God, but it represents humankind's best understanding of God's nature.
The Bible is an ancient book of human fables, legends, history and moral precepts.
No opinion.

	Literal word of God %	Inspired word of God %	Inspired word with errors %	Human Document %	Ancient Lit. %	No Opinion %
NATIONAL	31	24	22	7	10	6
Men	28	23	21	8	13	7
Women	34	26	22	6	7	5
Whites	29	25	23	8	10	5
Blacks	45	23	14	4	4	10
Protestants	37	27	22	5	5	4
Catholics	26	28	26	8	7	5

Findings are based on personal interviews with 2,556 adults nationwide during March 1988.

Source. Gallup Survey for the National Catholic Evangelization Association

The question of biblical inerrancy and authority has been debated for centuries and has never resulted in an absolute consensus of opinion on whether scriptures are historically reliable. Even today, exegetical scholars — interpreters of the original Greek or Hebrew texts — share diverse ideas about authorship and ways in which the Bible conveys literal, symbolic or moral teachings, and how scriptures should be understood in light of contemporary human experience.

Americans reflect this same diversity of opinion. Thirty-one percent feel the Bible is the "actual word of God and is to be taken literally, word for word," a view generally associated with fundamentalists. Biblical literalism is more prevalent among women than men (34% to 28%), and far more evident among blacks than whites (45% to 29%). A greater percentage of Protestants (37%) than Catholics (26%) understands scriptures literally, while only 11% of adults of "other" faiths ascribe to this view.

A fairly even distribution of responses holds for those who believe the Bible is the "inspired word of God," inerrant but "to be taken symbolically rather than literally." A total of 24% agree; especially women, whites and Catholics.

Nationally, 22% say the Bible is "the inspired word of God, but it may contain historical and scientific errors:" an idea some twentieth century theologians have used to "demythologize" the Bible. Men and women respond here in roughly the same numbers (21% to 22%), whereas blacks (14%), whites (23%), Protestants (22%) and Catholics (26%) differ somewhat.

The fewest numbers believe the Bible was not divinely inspired but "represents humankind's best understanding of God's nature." Seven percent of adults share this claim; roughly as many cited among demographic and religious groups.

Ten percent of Americans think that "the Bible is an ancient book of human fables, legends, history and moral precepts," a secular conviction that men (13%) are more likely to hold than women (7%), and whites (10%) more than blacks (4%). Twenty-five percent of persons of faiths other than Protestants (5%) and Catholics (7%) share this interpretation.

BELIEF IN MIRACLES WIDELY HELD

Question:
Please tell me how much you agree or disagree with [this] statement:

Even today miracles are performed by the power of God.

	Completely Agree %	Mostly Agree %	Mostly Disagree %	Completely Disagree %	Don't Know %
NATIONAL	51	29	9	6	5
Men	43	29	14	7	7
Women	58	29	5	5	3
Under 30 years	45	32	11	6	6
30-49 years	50	29	9	7	5
50 and older	56	27	8	4	5
Protestants	58	28	7	3	4
White Protestants	56	29	8	3	4
Black Protestants	73	22	4	1	*
Evangelicals	78	19	2	0	1
Non-evangelicals	41	36	12	5	6
Catholics	47	35	10	3	5
No religious preference	18	23	19	25	15

*Less than one percent.

Findings are based on personal interviews with 3,021 adutls nationwide during May 1988.

Source: Gallup Survey for *Times Mirror*

In one sense the question of miracles asks whether the laws of nature are absolutely uniform. To most Americans, God intervenes in a way that cannot be explained by natural law or empirical science. Eighty-two percent believe that God performs modern day miracles; a view most prevalent among women, non-whites, Protestants—especially Evangelicals—and persons over 50.

By 87% to 72% women are more likely than men to believe in miracles, although the gap narrows by age. Seventy-seven percent of adults under 30 agree that God performs miracles, compared to 79% of persons 30 to 49 and 83% of those over 50.

While majorities of all religious groups affirm miracles, strength of belief varies significantly. Fifty-eight percent of Protestants "completely agree" they believe in miracles, considerably more than Catholics at 47%. Taken together, however, percentages in agreement range closely, by 86% to 82%. Among Protestants 56% of whites attest unequivocally to miracles, far fewer than blacks at 73%. Seventy-eight percent of Evangelicals in strong agreement compare with the lesser percentage of Non-evangelicals at 41%.

A MEANINGFUL LIFE 'VERY IMPORTANT' TO MOST AMERICANS

Question:
How important to you is the belief that your life is meaningful or has a purpose?

	Very Important %	Fairly Important %	Fairly Unimportant %	Not Important %
NATIONAL	70	25	4	1
Men	63	31	4	2
Women	76	20	3	1
Whites	67	27	4	2
Non-whites	84	12	3	1
Experienced Change in Faith				
Yes	73	23	3	1
No	62	29	6	3
Degree of Change				
More faith	75	21	3	1
No change	65	27	5	3
Less faith	61	33	5	1

Findings are based on personal interviews with 1,042 adults nationwide during March 1985.

Source: Gallup Survey for the Religious Education Association of the United States and Canada

hilosopher Hannah Arendt stated that modern loss of faith and sense of meaning is ot religious in origin, but the result of exclusive concern with self rather than the soul r humanity in general. During a time sociologists observe a self-obsessive "personood" in America, 70% nevertheless believe it " very important" that life is meaningul or has a purpose. This finding is not surprising. Conscious knowledge that life is neaningless or purposeless is a difficult philosophical position for any population to old. But a small segment (5%) believes that life's meaning is unimportant.

Vomen and non-whites are more likely than men or whites to attach a high degree of mportance to a meaningful life, which suggests that white males are somewhat more lienated; that is, less likely to value a sense of inner purpose or meaning. In addition hose who report a change in their faith, or report greater faith now than at age 15, are nore likely than others to consider a life with meaning or purpose very important.

LARGE NUMBERS SAY HEAVEN AND HELL EXIST

Question:
Do you think there is a Heaven where people who had led good lives are eternally rewarded?

	Yes %	No %	Don't Know %
NATIONAL	71	21	8
Men	66	24	10
Women	75	20	5
Protestants	77	17	6
Catholics	73	17	10

Question:
Do you think there is a Hell, to which people who had led bad lives without being sorry are eternally damned?

	Yes %	No %	Don't Know %
NATIONAL	53	37	10
Men	50	37	13
Women	55	38	7
Protestants	61	30	9
Catholics	48	40	12

Findings are based on 1,003 interviews with adults nationwide during 1981.

Source: Gallup Poll

Seven in ten Americans (71%) believe there is a heaven where the good are eternally rewarded. The finding has been constant over the last thirty years, though according to the most recent survey, variations in belief hold across genders, religions and regions. More women than men believe in heaven by 75% to 66%, and while differences among Protestants and Catholics seem insignificant at 77% to 73%, the 30-year trend shows a steady decline among Catholics and an increase of Protestants who believe in heaven. Midwesterners and Southerners in particular are more likely to agree there is a heaven.

Asked whether they believe there is a hell where the unrepentant are eternally damned, fewer total respondents (53%) answer affirmatively. Gender differences are slight, with 50% of men and 55% of women saying there is a literal hell. Catholics are less likely than Protestants to believe in hell, by a margin of 48% to 61%.

Given traditional Catholic teachings on purgatory and the soul's heavenly reward, the results suggest many American Catholics differ from the church on the nature and meaning of eternal life.

SEVEN IN TEN BELIEVE IN LIFE AFTER DEATH

Question:
Do you believe that there life after death?

	Yes %	No %	Not Sure %
NATIONAL	71	16	13
Men	66	20	14
Women	76	12	12
Protestants	78	13	9
Catholics	71	14	15

The trend:

1988	71 %
1981	71
1980	67
1978	71
1975	69
1968	73
1965	75
1961	74
1957	74
1952	77
1948	68
1944	76

Latest findings are based on personal interviews with 2,556 adults nationwide during March 1988.

Source: Gallup Survey for the National Catholic Evangelization Association

Humankind has pondered the question of life after death since earliest recorded history. In recent times reports of near-death experiences have documented an extradimensional realm witnessed by those on the verge of passing from the body.

Current findings show that seven in ten Americans (71%) believe in life after death, a steady figure since 1944, with the exception of downtrends to 68% in 1948 and 67% in 1980.

By 76% to 66%, women are more likely than men to say there is an afterlife, though the margin of difference narrows in the category of uncertain respondents: 14% of men and 12% of women.

Protestants (78%) are somewhat more inclined than Catholics (71%) to affirm life after death. The trend on this measure reflects related findings on Catholic and Protestant beliefs about aspects of eternal life. Over the past thirty years fewer Catholics have expressed belief in the afterlife, but the reverse is the case for Protestants, due partly to the influence of evangelical Christianity and its emphasis on the hereafter.

EIGHTY PERCENT EXPECT THE LAST JUDGMENT

Question:
Please tell me how much you agree with [this] statement.

We will all be called before God at the judgment day to answer for our sins.

	Completely Agree %	Mostly Agree %	Mostly Disagree %	Completely Disagree %	No Opinion %
NATIONAL	52	28	8	6	6
Men	45	31	10	7	7
Women	59	25	7	5	4
Under 30 years	45	35	8	6	6
30-49 years	50	26	9	9	6
50 and older	60	24	8	4	4
Protestants	60	26	7	3	4
White Protestants	58	26	7	4	5
Black Protestants	66	27	4	1	2
Evangelicals	78	17	2	2	1
Non-evangelicals	45	33	10	5	7
Catholics	49	35	9	2	5
No religious preference	14	26	17	28	15

Findings are based on personal interviews with 3,021 adults nationwide during May 1988.

Source: Gallup Survey for *Times Mirror*

Jesus' parable of the last judgment (Matt. 25:31-46) prophesies the end of time, with all nations separated "as a shepherd separates the sheep from the goats" for a cosmic reckoning of human conduct on earth. The Book of Revelation narrates a more gruesome apocalypse that mirrors early Christians' persecution at the hands of the Roman Emperor Nero.

As a message of hope, most churches teach the end time as victory over sin and resurrection of the dead in the presence of a risen Lord. A remarkable 80% agree that they will be called before God on judgment day, an indication of the extent to which the idea is real and of ultimate consequence in the minds of Americans.

More women than men foresee a last judgment, by a margin of 84% to 76%. In terms of age, highest levels of belief occur among those 50 and older (84%), with persons 30 to 49 (76%) less likely to believe than adults under 30 (80%).

More Protestants than Catholics strongly affirm the last judgment by 60% to 49%, though total numbers in agreement are about even at 86% to 84%. A vast majority of black Protestants, 93%, expect a final reckoning, compared to 84% of white Protestants. Not surprisingly, almost all Evangelicals agree (95%) and thus signal a notable departure from Non-evangelicals (78%).

MAJORITY BELIEVE IN THE SECOND COMING

Question:

According to the Bible, Jesus promised to return to earth someday. Do you have serious doubts that this will happen, or have no doubts that this will happen?

	NATIONAL
Have serious doubts	10 %
Have some doubts	16
Have no doubts	62
Has already happened or is happening (volunteered)	1
No opinion	11
	100 %

The following table shows results by groups, based on those saying they have no doubts:

NATIONAL	62 %
Protestants	74
Baptist	80
Southern Baptist	80
Methodist	64
Lutheran	70
Presbyterian	66
Episcopalian	62
Catholics	59
18-24 years	61
25-29 years	58
30-49 years	59
50-64 years	65
65 and older	68

Findings are based on personal interviews with 2,669 adults nationwide during December 1982.

Source: Gallup Survey for the Robert Schuller Ministries

A solid majority of Americans (62%) harbor no doubts that Jesus will return to earth someday, as prophesied in the New Testament. Among those who say religion is very important in their lives, 79% believe in the Second Coming of Christ.

According to findings from a 1982 survey, about one-fourth of the total sample have some doubts (16%) or serious doubts (10%) about Jesus' return. Another 1% volunteer that the Second Coming has already taken place or is happening now.

A higher proportion of Protestants (74%) than Catholics (59%) anticipate Christ's coming, with Baptists and Southern Baptists (80% each) more likely to believe than Methodists (64%), Lutherans (70%), Presbyterians (66%) and Episcopalians (62%). And although young adults between 18 and 24 years tend to be less religious in a formal sense, they are as likely as persons 25 to 49 to say Jesus will return.

The expectations of early Christians was that the Second Coming would occur in their lifetime and had in one sense been fulfilled by the sufferings of martyrs such as Stephen (Acts 7:54-60). For nearly two thousand years, countless interpretations have been advanced on the meaning and imminence of Christ's return and Christian eschatology, a written and oral tradition based on apocalyptic Jewish prophecy.

AMERICANS REFLECT ON GOD'S IMAGES

Question:
There are many different ways of picturing God. We'd like to know the kinds of images you are most likely to associate with God.

> *Here is a card with sets of contrasting images. On a scale of 1-7 where would you place your image of God between the contrasting images?*
>
> *The first set of contrasting images shows Mother at 1 on the scale and Father at 7. If you image God as a Mother you would place yourself at 1. If you image God as a Father, you would place yourself at 7. If you image God as somewhere between Mother and Father, you would place yourself at 2, 3, 4, 5 or 6.*
>
> *Where would you place your image of God on the scale for. . .*

—SCALE POINTS—

	1 %	2 %	3 %	4 %	5 %	6 %	7 %		No Opinion
Mother	3	1	3	19	7	8	46	Father	13
Master	44	11	6	16	2	1	4	Spouse	16
Judge	35	9	8	20	4	2	7	Lover	15
Friend	24	6	6	24	5	3	18	King	14
Creator	33	6	4	35	2	2	5	Healer	13
Redeemer	37	8	6	25	2	2	4	Liberator	16

Findings are based on personal interviews with 1,509 adults during November 1984.

Source: Gallup Poll

As a contribution to the extensive research conducted by the Reverend Andrew M. Greeley and the National Opinion Research Center, The Gallup Organization repeated a question asked by NORC. This 4-item measurement on images of God predicts attitudes and behaviors that suggest Americans are rethinking creeds which narrow the scope of images.

Though a larger percentage (46%) pictures God as Father, 19% identify an image of God at the center of the scale and 3% view God as Mother. Greater numbers adhere to images of Master, Judge, Creator and Redeemer, as well as the more participatory image of God as Friend.

Detailed findings show that Evangelicals are far more likely than Non-evangelicals to see God as Father, Master, Judge, Creator and Redeemer. Among Non-evangelicals, responses are more evenly distributed across the scale.

In a separate survey conducted in 1985, majorities described God as "caring," "loving," and "all powerful" and "existing." However, these findings indicated that behind the overwhelming expression of belief in God, there was less than total certainty on all the items tested, including the question of existence.

MOST THINK THE DEVIL EXISTS

Question:
Which one of these statements comes closest to describing your feelings about the Devil?

1. *The Devil is a personal being who directs evil forces and influences people to do wrong.*

2. *The Devil is an impersonal force that influences people to do wrong.*

3. *The Devil does not exist, either as a being or a force.*

	A Personal Being %	An Impersonal Force %	Does Not Exist %	Don't Know %
NATIONAL	34	36	20	10
Men	31	35	23	11
Women	32	41	19	8
Catholics	32	41	19	8
Protestants	40	36	16	8
Southern Baptists	53	38	6	3
Baptists	52	36	6	6
Methodists	24	47	21	8
Lutherans	34	36	21	9

Findings are based on personal interviews with 1,553 adults nationwide during November 1978.

Source: Gallup Survey for *Christianity Today*

Americans are roughly divided evenly between those who think the Devil is "a personal being who directs evil forces and influences people to do wrong" (34%), and those who feel the Devil is "an impersonal force that influences people to do wrong" (36%). Another 20% believe the Devil does not exist, either as a being or a force, while 10% express no opinion.

Among denominations, Southern Baptists and Baptists are more likely to say the Devil is a personal being, with Methodists and Catholics prone to say it is an impersonal force. Lutherans and Methodists are most inclined to say the Devil does not exist.

In a 1981 survey conducted in 14 nations by GIRI for CARA and the European Value System Study Group, two-thirds of Americans (66%) said they believe in the Devil, against 28% who did not and 6% uncertain. The U.S. shared the highest percentage with Northern Ireland while citizens of Sweden, Denmark, France and West Germany most frequently denied the Devil's existence.

PUBLIC OPINION SPLIT ON EVOLUTION

Question:

Which of the statements on this card comes closest to describing your views about the origin and development of man?

> *A. God created man pretty much in his present form at one time within the last 10,000 years.*
>
> *B. Man has developed over millions of years from less advanced forms of life. God had no part in this process.*
>
> *C. Man has developed over millions of years from less advanced forms of life, but God guided this process, including man's creation.*
>
> *D. Other, don't know.*

	Creationism %	Evolution With God %	Evolution Without God %	Other, Don't Know %
NATIONAL	44	38	9	9
College (total)	30	50	15	5
Graduates	24	53	17	6
Incomplete	36	47	12	5
High School	49	35	7	9
Grade School	52	26	5	17
18-29 years	37	44	10	9
30-49 years	40	42	10	8
50 and over	53	30	7	10
Protestants	49	36	7	8
Catholics	38	47	8	7

Findings are based on personal interviews with 1,518 adults nationwide during July 1982.

Source: Gallup Survey for *Christianity Today*

Debate over human origins continues long after the famous Scopes trial in 1925. Gallup findings show the public evenly divided between believers in the biblical account of creation and evolution of the human species.

Forty-four percent said in 1982 that God created humans as they now exist within the last 10,000 years. Nine percent hold the view of evolution without God, while 38% agree that humans evolved from less advanced forms of life in an evolutionary process guided by God.

Evolutionists cite the evidence of data gathered during the past two centuries among the sciences: geology, paleontology, molecular biology and related fields of inquiry. Broadly, the theory of evolution states that the earth and physical universe are billions of years old, and that life forms developed gradually over time through a process of adaptation to their environments.

For creationists, who cite the book of Genesis, the earth and most life forms came into existence suddenly at some time within the last 10,000 years as a result of an act of God.

Analysis of the findings reveals:

- Persons with college training lean 2-to-1 in favor of evolution, but nearly one-third of the college segment believes the biblical account of creation. Graduates are more apt to believe in evolution.

- Adults under 30 years of age are about as likely to believe in creationism as those 30 to 49. People over 50 are more likely, however, to accept creationism.

- The views of Protestants and Catholics differ rather sharply, with Protestants leaning toward creationism by 49% to 43%, and Catholics siding with evolutionary theories by 55% to 38%.

EXTRATERRESTRIAL LIFE AFFIRMED BY 50%

Question:
Do you think there are people somewhat like ourselves living on other planets in the universe, or not?

	Yes %	No %	Not Sure %
1987	50	34	16
1978	51	33	16
1973	46	38	16
1966	34	46	20

Latest findings are based on telephone interviews with 527 adults nationwide during February 1987.

Source: Gallup Poll

Fifty percent of Americans share the belief that there are "people somewhat like ourselves living on other planets in the universe." Thirty-four percent are skeptical and 16% uncertain.

The findings are consistent with a 1986 National Science Foundation report stating 43% nationwide think it "likely" that some cited UFOs "are really space vehicles from other civilizations;" a notion used among New Agers to explain the intelligence responsible for the likes of Stonehenge, the Egyptian pyramids, and remains in Peru of the Machu Pichu.

Moreover, current Gallup figures are virtually unchanged from those recorded in a 1978 survey, suggesting the widely publicized New Age witness to extraterrestrial life has not significantly affected a belief held by half the citizenry over the last decade. However, the percentage of those believers is up considerably more now than in 1973 (46%) and 1966 (34%).

ONE IN FOUR BELIEVES IN REINCARNATION

Question:
Do you believe in reincarnation—that is, the birth of the soul in a new body after death, or not?

Adults

	Yes %	No %	No Opinion %
NATIONAL	23	67	10
18-24 years	30	61	9
25-29 years	29	61	10
30-49 years	21	68	11
50 and older	21	71	8
Protestants	21	68	11
Catholics	25	68	7

Findings are based on personal interviews with 1,003 adults nationwide during 1981.

Source: Gallup Poll

Teens

Yes	31 %
No	65
No Opinion	4
	100 %

Findings are based on telephone interviews with 503 teens 13 to 17 nationwide during March 1989.

Source: Gallup Youth Survey

About one American in four, 23%, say they believe in reincarnation—that their souls at death are born into a new human body or other form of life— what Plato called the transmigration of souls.The Gallup finding is surprising in light of the fact that eight in ten Americans give their religious preference broadly as Christian.

Involvement in organized religion nevertheless affects patterns of belief. About 17% of regular churchgoers report they believe in reincarnation, compared to 27% of those who do not attend regularly: an indication that the churched population is more likely to adhere to traditional Christian doctrine, which denies reincarnation, yet departs to some extent from doctrinal creeds. Furthermore, 47% for whom religion is "very" or "fairly" important believe in reincarnation.

Twenty-seven percent of Westerners believe in reincarnation, compared to 22% of those in the South, where evangelical Christianity is most pronounced and biblical doctrine is more likely to be held to the exclusion of other persuasions. The West Coast, on the other hand, has been most influenced by the New Age movement and Eastern religions, both of which include reincarnation as an article of belief.

In 1968 Gallup polled American adults on the question of reincarnation, although the survey did not include a definition of the term. That year 20% nationwide said they believed in reincarnation, statistically matching the 1981 figure.

According to a 1989 Gallup Youth Survey, 31% of teens believe in reincarnation and 65% do not. Among adults belief rises to 30% for persons 18 to 24 years old.

AMERICANS SKEPTICAL OF ASTROLOGY

Question:
What are your own views on astrology—do you believe in it, or not?

Believe in it	12 %
Don't believe in it	80
Don't know	8
	100%

Findings are based on telephone interviews with 1,204 adults nationwide during May 1988.

Source: Gallup Poll

Relatively few Americans (12%) believe in astrology; a system of meaning formulated among ancient Greeks, now understood to mean that movements of celestial bodies affect or determine human events and personalities. Eighty percent nationwide take no stock in astrology, while 8% are undecided. The figures reflect considerably more skepticism toward astrology than a decade ago, when a 1978 Gallup survey found 29% of adults believing in stars.

During 1988 Donald Regan's disclosures of astrology in the White House touched off a controversy concerning Nancy Reagan's consultations with an astrologer in planning the presidential schedule. In his autobiography Reagan confided that during his days as California's governor, he regularly read the astrology column.

A survey conducted in 1988 revealed that as many Americans today (25%) share this practice as in 1975 (23%). And more today, 85% to 76% in 1975, know the sign under which they were born.

Women are more likely to believe in astrology than men (16% to 9%), non-whites than whites (20% to 11%), and persons under 30 than those 50 and older (16% to 10%). Little difference obtains on the basis of formal education, however. Ten percent of college graduates believe in astrology, compared to 11% of adults who have attended but not graduated from college, and 14% with high school education.

Many find astrology compatible with traditional religious beliefs. A 1975 poll showed that as many churchgoers as non-churchgoers believe in astrology. This analysis was not made with the latest survey results.

TEENS TAKE STOCK OF THE SUPERNATURAL

Question:
Which of the following do you believe in—ghosts, the Loch Ness monster, Sasquatch (Bigfoot), witchcraft, ESP, clairvoyance, angels, astrology?

	National %	Male %	Female %	Ages 13-15 %	Ages 16-17 %
Angels	74	73	74	74	73
Astrology	58	53	64	60	56
ESP	50	54	46	47	54
Witchcraft	29	30	28	26	34
Bigfoot	22	33	11	22	24
Ghosts	22	28	16	19	25
Clairvoyance	21	24	19	15	30
Loch Ness Monster	16	22	10	16	16

	1988 %	1986 %	1984 %	1978 %
Angels	74	67	69	64
Astrology	58	52	55	40
ESP	50	46	59	67
Witchcraft	29	19	22	25
Bigfoot	22	16	24	40
Ghosts	22	15	20	20
Clairvoyance	21	19	28	25
Loch Ness Monster	16	13	18	31

Latest findings are based on telephone interviews with 506 teens 13 to 17 nationwide during June/July 1988.

Source: Gallup Youth Survey

More teens than ever believe in angels, but more also think that witchcraft exists, according to the latest Gallup Youth Survey. Overall, 95% of teens say they believe in at least one of the supernatural phenomena investigated in the survey.

Three teens in four (74%) say they believe in angels. Teens who attend church regularly (82%) are most likely to believe in the heavenly messengers, but two in three teens who are not regular church attenders (67%) also believe in their existence. Belief in angels has risen from 64% of teens in 1978 to the current level of 74%.

Currently, 29% of teens say they believe in witchcraft, compared to 25% in 1978. No difference is found in witchcraft belief according to the religious practices of teens.

Levels of teens' belief in astrology have varied over the years, and now 58% say they think that movement of the celestial bodies influences their lives. By comparison only 40% held similar beliefs in 1978.

Young women are more likely than young men to ask, "What sign are you?" by a margin of 64% to 53%. The scientific community has dismissed astrology, and above-average students (54%) are less likely than those who are doing average or below-average work in school (63%) to believe in astrology.

ESP — (extrasensory perception) — is deemed possible by half the teens (50%). Belief in ESP is highest among young men (54%) and teens who are 16 and older (54%). Clairvoyance, the ability to see into the future or beyond normal sensory range, is thought possible by 21% of the teens. Belief in clairvoyance also is greater among young men (24%) and older teens (30%). The proportion of teens who believe in ESP has dropped, from 54% in 1978 to the current 50%. In the same period the proportion of teens claiming the existence of clairvoyance has fallen, from 30% to 21%.

Ghosts are more than Halloween fantasies to 22% of teens, about as many who believe that Bigfoot may be stalking the Pacific Northwest or the Tibetan foothills. But today only 16% hold out the belief that a prehistoric creature called "Nessie" roams the depths of Loch Ness in Scotland. Young men are most likely to believe in Bigfoot (33%), ghosts (22%) and the Loch Ness monster (22%). Young women are far more skeptical: only 11% believe in Bigfoot, 10% in the Loch Ness monster and 16% in ghosts.

Belief in ghosts has remained steady between 1978 (20%) and 1988 (22%); however, during the same period the number of Bigfoot believers has dropped from 40% to 22%, while the ranks of those who hope someday to see the Loch Ness monster have fallen from 31% to 16%.

II. Religious Practices

Although 94% of American adults believe in God, lesser but substantial majorities engage in the conscious practice of faith. A striking 87% agree "completely" or "mostly" that they never doubt the existence of God, a claim made by 29% of those with no religious preference. Eighty-eight percent nationwide pray to God, while 76% agree that prayer is "an important part" of their daily lives—findings that suggest the enormous extent of private piety in the U.S., which coexists with notable expressions of self-reliance.

Forty-five percent in 1987 said they rely on themselves to solve life problems, compared to 36% who depend "more on an outside power, such as God." Seventeen percent volunteered both answers. However, when asked in a separate survey more concrete questions about actual problems, most Americans said they turn to God with specific and practical intentions. Eighty percent pray through crises, while 64% read the Bible or inspirational literature. Forty-eight percent say they pray or read the Bible when depressed, and of those, virtually all (94%) report effective results.

But far fewer are committed to ongoing or systematic reading of scriptures. Eleven percent in 1986 read the Bible daily; twice as many (22%) read scriptures weekly, and 14% monthly, while 22% never read the Bible — figures roughly equal to those recorded in 1982 and 1978. Only 42% can name five of the Ten Commandments, with 43% unable to name the four Gospels. Four in ten Americans (42%) know that Jesus delivered the Sermon on the Mount, compared to seven in ten (70%) who know he was born in Bethlehem, a fact recounted widely every year in the oral tradition of Christmas. Biblical illiteracy in America stems partly from ignorance of scriptures, but also from functional illiteracy among an estimated 27 million Americans, about one adult in five.

Still, significant numbers report involvement in religious group activity such as Bible study. In 1985 about 46 million U. S. adults (26%) took part in Bible study, the same figure recorded in 1983. A related survey in 1988 found that nearly as many (22%) are involved in small groups outside the church, such as Bible or prayer meetings. Of that proportion 49% attended regularly. Charismatic groups, often gathered to pray and study scriptures, drew 3% of the population in 1985 and 1983. By 1988 one in ten Americans (9%) had attended a charismatic group within the last two years.

While Protestants in 1988 were more likely than Catholics to attend small Bible study and prayer meetings (27% to 15%), Catholics have stepped up these activities considerably, and in 1986 were more likely to attend Catholic functions, prayer meetings and outreach programs than in 1977.

If four in ten Americans (39%) in 1984 said that Christians should stress personal spiritual growth, public exercise of religious values has become increasingly apparent. Volunteerism has gained ground in the last decade, with 39% involved in charitable activities, up from 27% in 1977. A vast majority of adults (86%) would want their children to receive religious instruction, along with 73% of the unchurched population. Clearly, Americans are seeking meaningful and common avenues for the practice of faith.

MANY REPORT DAILY PRAYER

Question:
Please tell me how much you agree or disagree with [this] statement.

Prayer is an important part of my daily life.

	Completely Agree %	Mostly Agree %	Mostly Disagree %	Completely Disagree %	Don't Know %
NATIONAL	41	35	17	6	1
	76		23		

Findings are based on personal interviews with 4,244 adults nationwide during April/May 1987.

Source: Gallup Survey for *Times Mirror*

Question:
Do you every pray to God?

	Yes %	No %	Don't Know %
NATIONAL	88	11	1
Men	83	16	1
Women	93	6	1
White	88	11	1
Black	93	7	*
Hispanic	89	9	2
Protestants	95	5	*
Catholics	91	8	1
Other	71	26	3
Churched	97	3	*
Unchurched	77	21	2

*Less than one percent.

Findings are based on personal interviews with 2,556 adults nationwide during March 1988.

Source: Gallup Survey for the National Catholic Evangelization Association

A leading indicator of the nation's religious mood, the practice of prayer in the U.S. reveals a deep spiritual thirst among Americans. Seventy-six percent agree "completely" or "mostly" that "prayer is an important part of everyday life."

Most apt to cite the importance of daily prayer are women (82%), non-whites (90%), those without a high school degree (84%), persons over 50 (85%) and Evangelicals or self-described born-again Christians (93%).

Groups less inclined to stress daily prayer are men (69%), college graduates (65%), persons under 30 (68%), and Jews (36%). Catholics and Protestants at 80% each say that prayer is an important daily exercise.

To a related question on incidence of prayer, a large majority of adults, 88%, say they pray to God; 11% never pray. Incidence of prayer is high in absolute terms, even among the unchurched (77%), but nearly universal (97%) among those who are churched. Women and blacks, the strongest practioners of prayer at 93% each, compare with their opposite numbers by 83% of men, 88% of whites and 89% of Hispanics. Vast majorities of Protestants (95%) and Catholics (91%) pray to God, along with a substantial percentage of persons of other faiths (71%).

In 1948 ninety percent of Americans said they practiced prayer at some time in their lives. The figure held steady at 92% in 1952 and 1965, 89% in 1978, 88% in 1982 and 87% in 1985.

A 1952 poll showed 42% of Americans prayed twice a day or more; roughly the same proportion of 41% in 1965, which preceded a drop to 27% in 1978. In 1982 30% said they prayed more than once a day, comparable to the 31% in 1985.

A survey conducted in 1984 for the Christian Broadcasting Network indicated the most prevalent subject of prayer to be health or healing for family or friends, cited by 22% of those who had prayed within the past 24 hours. Nineteen percent asked for help or guidance, 15% prayed for their family, 12% prayed to give thanks, 7% offered general prayer, 6% prayed for others, 6% for world peace, and 5% for self-improvement.

ONE-THIRD OF ADULTS READ BIBLE WEEKLY OR MORE

Question:
How often do you read the Bible?

	Daily %	Weekly %	Monthly %	Less than monthly %	Never %
NATIONAL*	11	22	14	26	22

*"Can't say," 5% nationwide, omitted

	1986 %	1982 %	1978 %
More than once a day	1	2	1
Daily	10	13	11
2 or 3 times a week	9	9	8
Weekly	13	9	10
2 or 3 times a month	6	5	4
Once a month	8	7	7
Less than once a month	26	25	28
Never read	22	24	24
Can't say	5	6	7
	100%	100%	100%

Latest findings are based on personal interviews with 1,559 adults nationwide during October 1986.

Source: Gallup Poll public service, in conjunction with the Laymen's National Bible Committee

Teen Bible Reading

	Daily %	At least weekly %	At least monthly %	Less than monthly %	Rarely or never %
NATIONAL	10	30	18	22	20

Findings are based on telephone interviews with 504 teenagers 13 to 17, nationwide during May/June 1986.

Source: Gallup Youth Survey

One-third of adult Americans (33%) read the Bible at least once a week, with one in nine a daily reader. One in seven (14%) reads the Bible at least once a month, about one in four (26%) less than monthly, and one in five (22%) never reads scriptures. These figures are virtually unchanged from earlier surveys.

The Bible is near the top of many teens' book lists. A majority of American teens (58%) say they read the Bible at least monthly, according to a Gallup Youth Survey. This finding represents a slight increase in Bible reading since 1983, when 55% of all teens reported reading scriptures at least monthly.

One teen in ten (10%) reports daily Bible reading. Thirty percent of teens say they read the Bible at least once a week, and 18% at least monthly. Twenty -two percent say they read it less often than once a month. One teen in five (20%) rarely or never reads the Bible.

KNOWLEDGE OF BIBLE MEAGER

Question:
Can you name five of the Ten Commandments?

	All five correct %	Four correct %	Three correct %	Two correct %	One correct %	Don't know %
NATIONAL	42	21	14	8	2	13

Findings are based on personal interviews with 1,553 adults nationwide during November 1978.

Source: Gallup Survey for *Christianity Today*

Question:
Will you tell me the names of the first four books of the New Testament of the Bible—that is, the four Gospels?

	All four correct %	Three correct %	Two correct %	One correct %	None correct %	Don't know %
NATIONAL	46	4	2	2	3	43

Question:
Who delivered the Sermon on the Mount?

	Jesus %	Incorrect answer %	Don't know %
NATIONAL	42	24	34

Question:
Where was Jesus born?

	Bethlehem %	Incorrect answer %	Don't know %
NATIONAL	70	17	13

Findings are based on personal interviews with 1,509 adults nationwide during December 1982.

Source: Gallup Survey for the Robert H. Schuller Ministries

Although the Bible is the world's best seller, comparatively few adults seem familiar with important parts of it, due in part to widespread illiteracy in America. But many of the college educated and religiously involved know little of basic biblical facts.

Forty-five percent nationwide can name fewer than five of the Ten Commandments, the case also for 41% of the college trained and for 47% with a religious preference. Women, Catholics, Midwesterners, Southerners and persons 30 to 49 are more likely than their counterparts to know at least five of the Ten Commandments.

A total of 46% correctly state all four Gospels of the New Testament: Matthew, Mark, Luke and John. Among groups, women, Lutherans, Southerners and college graduates most frequently cite each of the four accurately.

Forty-two percent of American adults know that Jesus delivered the Sermon on the Mount (Matt. 5:1-7:29; Luke 6:20-49), with little significant differences among population groups, except the relatively high proportions of college graduates and Southerners.

Seventy percent of Americans know that Jesus was born in Bethlehem: especially women, Presbyterians, Episcopalians and persons over 65.

On the whole adults who are married and located in the Bible Belt demonstrate greater knowledge of the Bible.

FEW DOUBT GOD'S EXISTENCE

Question:
Please tell me how much you agree with [this] statement:

I never doubt the existence of God.

	Completely agree %	Mostly agree %	Mostly disagree %	Completely disagree %	No opinion %
NATIONAL	63	24	7	4	2
Men	55	28	10	5	2
Women	71	20	5	2	2
Under 30 years	58	27	9	4	2
30-49 years	60	24	9	5	2
50 and older	70	22	4	2	2
Protestants	69	22	5	2	2
White Protestants	69	22	5	2	2
Black Protestants	72	21	5	2	*
Evangelicals	85	12	1	1	1
Non-evangelicals	58	29	8	2	3
Catholics	62	27	7	2	2
No religious preference	29	30	20	15	6

*Less than one percent.

Findings are based on personal interviews with 3,021 adults nationwide during May 1988.

Source: Gallup Survey for *Times Mirror*

René Descartes was accused of heresy for questioning God's existence in meditations he published in 1641 to prove the reality of God by radical doubt. The role of doubt has fueled theological debate since the seventeenth century, when the new sciences made reason the criterion of faith rather than authority of the church or scriptures.

In the U.S. today, reason is more a matter of self-reliance than a means to doubt God or certainties that foster the social and moral stability Americans seek. Eighty-seven percent of adults say they never doubt the existence of God, a view held among more women than men by 91% to 83%.

While majorities of all age groups report high levels of faith, older Americans are least likely to doubt God's existence. Ninety-two percent of persons 50 or more make this claim, as compared to 84% of those 30 to 49 and 85% under 30.

About as many Catholics (89%) as Protestants (91%) agree they never doubt that God exists, with little differences among white Protestants (91%), black Protestants (93%), and Evangelicals (97%). An overwhelming majority of Non-evangelicals agree (87%). Importantly, six in ten (59%) Americans with no religious preference say they never doubt the existence of God.

MORE RELY ON SELF THAN GOD

Question:
Do you rely more on yourself to solve the problems of life, or more on an outside power, such as God?

More on self	45 %
Outside power	36
Both (volunteered)	17
No opinion	2
	100 %

Reliance on Self or God

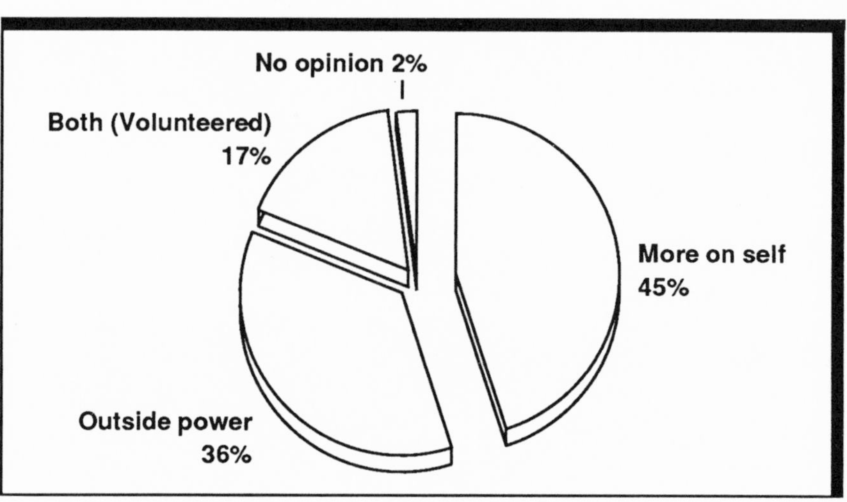

Findings are based on telephone interviews with 511 adults nationwide during May 1987.

Source: Gallup Survey for the Christian Broadcasting Network, Inc.

Asked whether they rely "more on yourself to solve the problems of life, or more on an outside power, such as God," 45% chose "self" as an answer, compared to 36% who said, "outside power." Another 17% said they called upon both.

The greatest disparities appeared between college graduates and those who did not go beyond high school, and between Evangelicals and Non-evangelicals. Of those who completed college, 61% said they relied primarily on themselves, compared to 30% of those whose formal education ended with high school. By contrast, only 22% of the college graduates staked their faith in an "outside power" to solve problems, against 49% of the high school graduates.

Evangelicals, at 56%, were the most likely to choose a higher power, while 59% of Non-evangelicals said they depend on the self.

AMERICANS STEP UP VOLUNTEERISM

Question:
Do you, yourself, happen to be involved in any charity or social service activities, such as helping the poor, the sick or the elderly?

(Percent saying yes)

	1987 %	1977 %	Point change
NATIONAL	39	27	+12
Men	42	24	+18
Women	36	29	+7

National Trend

(Percent saying yes)

1987	39 %
1986	36
1984	31
1982	29
1977	27

Latest findings are based on telephone interviews with 503 adults nationwide during May 1987

Source: Gallup Poll

Despite the high mobility of families in the U.S., the increase of women in the work force and charges that Americans are building a society of consumers, volunteerism continues to flourish in this nation.

As many as four in ten adults (39%) report formal or informal involvement in charitable activities such as helping the underprivileged, the infirm or elderly. The current figure represents the high point in a ten year trend recorded since 1977, when 27% volunteered charitable work.

The proportion of both male and female volunteers has grown over the last decade, but the gain has been more pronounced among men — up eighteen points — compared to seven points for women.

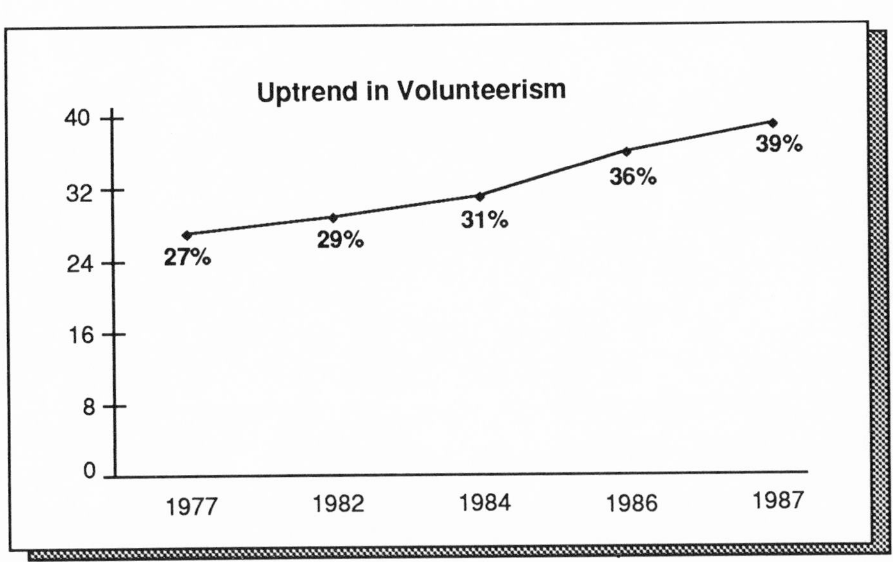

RELIGIOUS TRAINING FOR CHILDREN STRONGLY FAVORED

Question:
Would you want a child of yours to receive any religious instruction?

	Yes %	No %	No opinion %
NATIONAL	86	7	7
Men	83	9	6
Women	88	6	6
Whites	86	8	6
Blacks	87	7	6
Hispanics	80	10	10
Protestants	90	5	5
Catholics	91	4	5
Churched	96	2	2
Unchurched	73	14	13
Respondents with children 4-18	90	6	4

Findings are based on personal interviews with 2,556 adults nationwide during March 1988.

Source: Gallup Survey for the National Catholic Evangelization Association

During a time when children's spiritual development is growing ever more complex, a vast majority of Americans, 86%, say they would want a child of theirs to receive religious instruction. Ninety percent with children agree. Generally, the consensus is strongest in midwestern and southern states of the Bible Belt.

By a margin of 83% to 88%, men are somewhat less likely than women to stress religious instruction for youth, with whites (86%) and blacks (87%) in equal numbers and Hispanics, largely Catholic, at 80%.

While majorities across all demographic strata would choose religious training for a child, the preference is almost universal among churchgoers (96%). As many Protestants (90%) as Catholics (91%) favor such training.

RELIGIOUS SPECIAL PURPOSE GROUPS OUTSIDE CHURCH DRAW ONE IN FIVE

Question:
In the last years did you attend a prayer group, Bible study, or other religious group which meets somewhere other than a church?

	Yes %	No %
NATIONAL	22	78
Protestants	27	73
Catholics	15	85
Other	25	75

Question:
Did you attend on a regular basis, occasionally, or only once?

(Based on respondents who attended religious groups outside church in last two years.)

	Regular basis %	Occasionally %	Only once %	Don't know %
NATIONAL	49	45	1	5
Protestants	39	47	13	1
Catholics	22	45	33	*
Other	44	51	5	*

*Less than one percent.

Findings are based on personal interviews with 2,556 adults nationwide during March 1988.

Source: Gallup Survey for the National Catholic Evangelization Association

More than one in five Americans (22%) have attended a special purpose group such as Bible study, prayer or similar religious meeting outside a church or synagogue in the past two years. In light of a 1985 Gallup survey measuring *involvement* in such groups, 1988 attendance levels suggest consistent activity among participants, especially Protestants now at 27%.

By 25% to 19%, women show greater interest than men in fellowship outside the church, which also draws more persons between the ages of 25 and 29 attending at 26%, compared to 21% of those 18 to 24 and 30 to 49, and 22% of persons over 50. In addition attendance among Hispanics (29%) is somewhat higher than whites (22%) or blacks (20%). At 25% each, Southerners and Westerners are more likely than persons from the East (16%) and Midwest (21%) to take part in religious group meetings.

About half of group participants (49%) attend "on a regular basis," while nearly as many (45%) do so "occasionally," with Protestants (47%) and Catholics (45%) in roughly the same numbers on an occasional basis. Regular attendance levels, however, show Protestants more involved than Catholics by 39% to 22%. A sharp increase appears among "other" attendees, with 44% regularly and 51% occasionally at group meetings outside the church or synagogue.

RELIGIOUS ACTIVITIES GAIN NUMBERS

Question:
Which, if any, of these are you involved in, or do you practice?

	1985	Projection to millions of adults 1985*	1983	Projection to millions of adults 1983*
Bible study groups	26 %	46 million	26 %	43 million
Religious education	21	37	19	34
Prayer and meditation groups	18	32	17	30
Witnessing	14	25	13	23
Missionary work	10	18	8	14
Evangelism	9	16	9	16
Healing	6	11	5	9
Prophecy	4	7	4	7
Speaking in tongues	3	4	4	4
Charismatic movement	3	4	3	5

*Source: Current Population Reports, Projections of the Population of the United States

Latest findings are based on telephone interviews with 1,034 adults nationwide during April 1985.

Source: Gallup Survey for the Christian Broadcasting Network, Inc.

Four adults in ten (41%) have recently taken part in one or more of the religious activities listed above, while six in ten (59%) report no involvement. Protestants are far more likely to participate in the activities tested, by a total of 50% as compared to 29% of the Catholics surveyed.

Evangelicals and Non-evangelicals differ markedly in degree of involvement. Forty-three percent of Evangelicals surveyed engaged in prayer groups for example, compared to 13% of Non-evangelicals.

Interestingly, younger adults (18 to 29 years) — though customarily less involved in organized religion than their elders — show nearly the same degree of involvement as older adults in most activities.

Women are much more likely than men to take part in religious activities (45% to 35%), especially Bible study and prayer groups. In the charismatic movement, however, men and women participate equally. Moreover, those living in the Midwest and the South report higher levels of involvement than their counterparts in the East and West.

Participation Trends

After an apparent upturn in participation between 1978 and 1983, levels of involvement show a levelling out in the 1985 survey. In addition the proportion involved in one or more of the ten activities held at 41%.

MORE CATHOLICS SPIRITUALLY ACTIVE

Question:
By any chance, have you, yourself, done any of the following within the last 30 days?

Catholic Religious Activities

	1986 %	1977 %	Change from 1977
Meditated	39	32	+7 pts
Said (prayed) the Rosary	38	36	+2
Attended Catholic social function	33	21	+12
Read the Bible	32	23	+9
Gone to confession	23	18	+5
Attended a meeting of Catholic organization	17	10	+7
Attended a prayer meeting	12	8	+4
Participated in a Catholic action or outreach program	7	4	+3
Made a retreat	4	2	+2
Attended a spiritual conference	3	2	+1
Attended a marriage encounter session	2	3	-1

Findings are based on nationwide surveys conducted in 1977 and 1986.

Source: Gallup Survey for the Catholic Press Association

Although the level of weekly attendance at Mass among Catholics has changed little over the last decade, the number involved in Bible study, meditation, and other religious activities has grown substantially.

In part, the trend on group activity represents the Catholic manifestation of moderate religious revival in America today, which may be taking place without formal ties to the Church and in the midst of religious relocation. Further, because bishops have become more involved in the pastoral process — particularly with the peace pastoral on disarmament — Catholics have responded with enthusiasm toward the Church's statements on spiritual health and social justice. Their response, however, has done little to stem the tide of disaffection from less popular teachings on marriage and the role of women.

Group Activities Up

In a 1977 survey conducted for the Catholic Press Association, 23% of Catholics said they had read the Bible within the previous thirty days. In the 1987 poll the figure rose to 32%, up nine percentage points.

The percentage who attended Catholic social functions during a thirty-day test period increased twelve points, with meditation up seven points. A similar gain occurred in the proportion who attended meetings of Catholic organizations. Gains appeared also in percentages of Catholics who have gone to confession, attended prayer meetings, and participated in Catholic action or outreach programs.

NINE PERCENT HAVE ATTENDED CHARISMATIC GROUPS

Question:
In the last two years, have you attended a charismatic religious group, that is, one including gifts of the spirit?

	Yes %	No %	Don't know %
NATIONAL	9	89	2
Churched	12	87	1
Unchurched	4	94	2

Question:
Did you attend on a regular basis, occasionally, or only once?

(Based on those who attended a charismatic religious group in the last two years.)

	Regular basis %	Occasionally %	Once %	Don't know %
NATIONAL	35	48	17	*
Churched	41	44	15	*
Unchurched	16	62	22	0

*Less than one percent.

Findings are based on personal interviews with 2,556 adults nationwide during March 1988.

Source: Gallup Survey for the National Catholic Evangelization Association

In the past two years one in eleven adults (9%) has attended a charismatic religious group; that is, a group celebrating "gifts of the spirit" such as speaking in tongues, spiritual healing and prophecy.

Among churchgoing Americans 12% attend charismatic meetings, compared to 4% of unchurched respondents. Women and men attend equally (9%), though blacks (13%) and Hispanics (11%) are more inclined than whites (8%) to say they take part in charismatic activities. By region, Southerners are most likely to attend a charismatic group.

Of those who have attended one in three (35%) goes regularly, nearly half (48%) occasionally, and 17% only once. Churched respondents are more likely to attend on a regular basis than the unchurched. However, the sample of unchurched respondents on which this finding is based is small, and interpretation of it should be made cautiously.

In contrast to results from the companion question, women are far more likely than men to attend *regularly* by 41% to 28%. Most frequent attendees also include Hispanics, Southerners and Westerners, and persons over 50 years of age.

SPIRITUAL GROWTH NAMED FIRST CHRISTIAN PRIORITY

Question:
Regardless of whether or not you consider yourself a Christian, which one of these actions would you say should be the top priority of Christians?

	National %	Protestants %	Catholics %
Concentrate on the spiritual growth of one's family and self	39	37	43
Help to win the world for Jesus Christ (evangelism)	27	35	18
Support causes to improve the entire community	15	12	17
Strengthen the local church	6	6	7
Influence local, state and national legislation on important issues	5	4	7
No opinion	8	6	8
	100 %	100 %	100 %

Findings are based on personal interviews with 1,522 adults nationwide during November 1984.

Source: Gallup Survey for the Robert H. Schuller Ministries

Christians' top priority should be spiritual growth, according to recent findings that placed this item over evangelism, supporting community causes, strengthening the local church, and influencing legislation.

Among religious groups priorities depend largely on identification with liberals or conservatives and with Evangelicals or Non-evangelicals. Conservatives put evangelism first, while liberals think spiritual growth should be the first priority. A similar pattern is found among Evangelicals and Non-evangelicals.

Priorities differ also among Catholics and Protestants, with Catholics placing far less emphasis on evangelism than their opposite numbers.

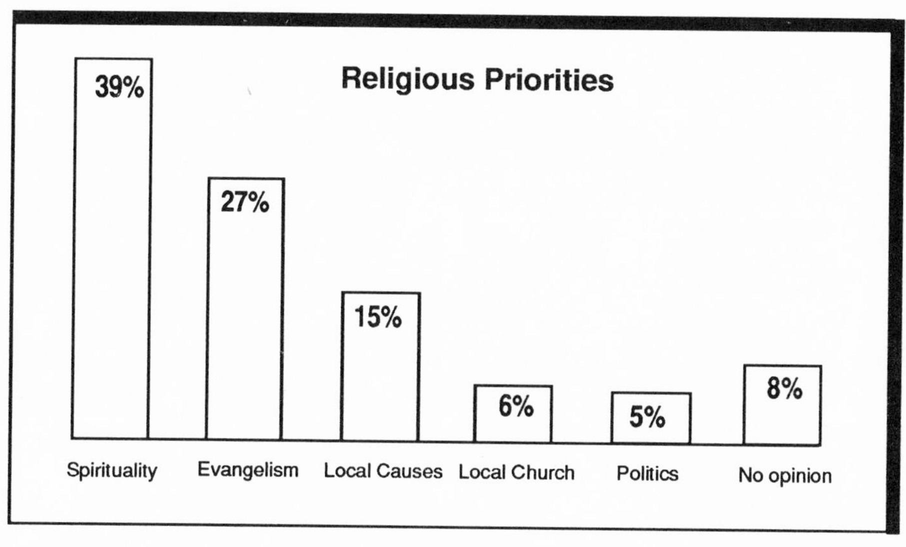

EIGHT IN TEN PRAY THROUGH CRISES

Question:
When you are faced with a problem or crisis, to which of the following kinds of support would you likely turn for help?

Share it with family.
Share it with close friends.
Discuss it with a class or a group in your church or synagogue.
Work it through on your own.
Read the Bible or other inspirational literature.
Seek help from a religious counselor.
Seek other professional counseling.
Seek help from a support group.
Pray about it.

Sources of Support	NATIONAL %	Men %	Women %	White %	Non-white %
Share with family	87	86	88	86	88
Prayer	80	74	86	78	94
Work it through on your own	80	85	75	80	79
Share with close friends	73	69	77	74	68
Read Bible/ inspirational literature	64	56	72	61	87
Religious counselor	40	35	46	38	55
Other professional counselor	31	28	34	31	35
Support group	26	22	29	24	34
Discuss with class or group in church or synagogue	23	17	27	21	33

Note: Totals add to more than 100% due to multiple responses.

Findings are based on telephone interviews with 1,042 adults during March 1985.

Source: Gallup Survey for the Religious Education Association of the United States and Canada

When faced with a problem or crises, adults most typically seek support from their families (87%). Eighty percent say they work out problems on their own, and 73% consult friends. Importantly, 80% pray and 64% turn to the Bible or inspirational literature. Formal sources of support such as religious counselors (40%), professional counselors (31%), support groups (26%) or religious groups (23%) figure in less frequently.

Patterns of response differ widely between genders, with women less inclined to isolate themselves in critical times and more prone to relational forms of support: friends, religious or support groups and counselors. Women also show greater likelihood to read the Bible and to pray about problems.

Similarly, non-whites are more likely than whites to seek counsel from groups, religious counselors, inspirational reading, and especially prayer.

PRAYER, BIBLE READING CITED BEST CURES FOR DEPRESSION

Question:
Please tell me whether you frequently or occasionally do the following when you feel discouraged or depressed.

(Based on the 81% who are ever depressed or discouraged)

	Frequently or occasionally engage in these activities %	Very or somewhat effective %
Spend more time alone, with a hobby, TV, reading, or listening to music	77	84
Seek out friends to talk with	68	90
Seek out family members to talk with	66	88
Eat more/less	64	31
Spend more time in prayer, meditation or reading the Bible	48	94
Spend more time in exercising	40	92
Shop more, spend money	31	47
Spend more hours at work	29	77
Seek out pastor, religious leader	27	87
Spend more time sleeping	26	59
Seek help from a doctor or professional counselor	14	71
Drink more alcohol	10	37
Rely more heavily on medication	6	58

Findings are based on telephone interviews with 1,007 adults nationwide during October 1986.

Source: Gallup Survey for the Christian Broadcasting Network, Inc.

n a 1986 survey eight in ten Americans (81%) reported bouts with depression, which best-selling psychiatrist M. Scott Peck says often accompanies mental and spiritual growth needed to adapt successfully to life events.

While most turn to a hobby, television, reading, or music to overcome depression, spiritual activities — prayer, meditation and Bible reading — are cited as the most effective means for dealing with depressive disorder. Following these are coping strategies such as exercise, talking with friends and family, seeking out a religious professional, increasing work hours, and consulting a doctor or psychologist. Comparatively ineffective patterns are said to be sleeping, relying on medication, altering spending and eating habits, and drinking alcohol.

Additional findings showed:

Ten percent of adults find themselves depressed or discouraged most of the time or quite often, while 44% say occasionally, and 26% almost never or never. Women are slightly more likely than men to report depression most of the time or quite often. Young adults (18 to 29) are more inclined to cite these responses than are older persons.

Income and education levels are factors indicating persons in lower economic groups and with little formal education are the most likely to experience depression on a frequent basis.

Of those who feel depressed on occasion (81%) — that is, excluding the 19% who say "never"— 2% say duration of depression tends to last "very long;" for another 9%, "fairly long," and 87% "not at all long."

Among those with "very" or "fairly long" depressions, gender differences are minimal, but a higher proportion of younger than older adults and more non-whites than whites offer these responses. Length of depression, like frequency, is closely related to income and education levels.

Money and bills, job related, family and health problems are volunteered most often as causes of depression or discouragement, followed by general frustrations, problems with children, the state of the economy, world affairs, and one's social life.

III. Church and Synagogue

The year 1988 marked the greatest level of disaffection in the five-decade history of Gallup surveys of church and synagogue membership. Sixty-five percent of the U.S. population reported membership — the lowest percentage recorded since Gallup's first membership audit in 1937 — with the proportion of unchurched Americans up slightly from 41% in 1978 to 44% in 1988. (The unchurched are defined as those who are not members of a church or have not attended services in the previous six months other than for special religious holidays, weddings, funerals or the like.)

Over the past two years serious declines in membership have occurred among young adults, Catholics and minority groups in particular. The percentage of blacks on membership rolls plunged from 75% in 1986 to 66% in 1988. Hispanic membership fell from 68% to 56%. For the first time as likely as Protestants to be church members, Catholics at 81% in 1986 dropped to 72% in 1988, the same figure recorded for Protestants both years. During that time membership for adults 18 to 29 years old took a downturn from 63% in 1986 to 55% in 1988. Attendance held steady among these groups, indicating their recent and notable trend toward religious relocation.

In terms of preference, one of the most constant measures of the spiritual climate, an estimated nine in ten Americans give a religious group identity. Regardless of configurations on membership, the declining Protestant majority (56%) has remained twice the size of the growing Catholic communion (28%) since the late 1970s. The rising proportion of Mormons in this country (2%) equals that of Jews (2%), whose numbers have dropped, while self-described evangelical or born-again Christians (33%) comprise one-third of the national population across denominations.

Preference notwithstanding, religious individualism persists within organized group loyalties. Seventy-six percent nationwide agreed in 1988 that a person can be "a good Christian of Jew" without attending church or synagogue. A total of 80% felt that "one should arrive at his or her religious beliefs independently of any church or synagogue," a figure roughly matching that cited in 1978. Supported by related findings on Americans' beliefs and practices, these results suggest a growing trend toward religious privacy, which correlates with the drop in membership.

Despite the stability of national attendance (42%), Americans have grown increasingly dissatisfied with religious institutions. The percentage expressing "a great deal" or "quite a lot" of confidence in organized religion (59%) has declined steadily since 1985, although a striking 80% in 1988 agreed "strongly" or "moderately" that churches and synagogues have grasped "the real spiritual nature of religion." But more specific results showed Americans more critical of the priorities and direction of organized religion. Fifty-nine percent said churches were too concerned with organizational issues, up from 51% in 1978. Forty-one percent agreed that churches were not enough concerned about social justice, compared to 35% in 1978. (Only 4% have experienced racism or ethnic exclusion in churches or synagogues, typically homogeneous and thus segregated *ipso facto*.) Moreover, a minority up from 27% in 1978 to 32% in 1988 felt the morality taught in churches is too restrictive.

The picture of the Catholic Church is somewhat more detailed and may help explain the recent drop in membership. A 1986 poll suggests American Catholics approve of their church as a whole, but majorities question its teachings on contraception, divorce and women's ordination. In addition Catholics' approval rating of Pope John Paul II fell significantly from 80% in 1979 to 69% in 1987.

While discontent colors the religious mood in America, satisfaction with the church in 1981 was greater than in many industrialized countries. That year an international Gallup survey of Americans and the citizens of thirteen western European nations found that 73% of U.S. adults felt their churches were meeting spiritual needs, the highest among the nations polled.

PROTESTANTS HOLD STRONG MAJORITY IN AMERICA

Question:
What is your religious preference — Protestant, Roman Catholic, Jewish, Mormon, or an Orthodox Church such as the Greek or Russian Orthodox Church?

Protestant	56 %
Roman Catholic	28
Jewish	2
Mormon (The Church of Jesus Christ of Latter Day Saints)	2
Orthodox Church	*
Other	2
None	10

*Less than one percent.

Religious Preference

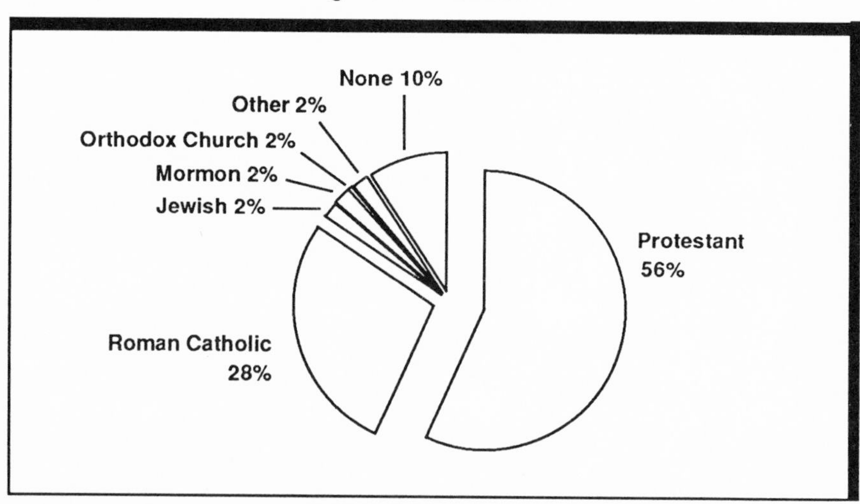

Findings are based on personal and telephone interviews with 15,460 adults nationwide during 1988.

Source: Gallup Poll

Roughly nine in ten American adults state a specific religious preference. A 56% majority gives its preference as Protestant, a faith that sociologist of religion Max Weber believed was the decisive force in shaping the nation's work ethic and economic system. The Catholic communion claims 28% nationwide, a proportion that has increased from 20% since 1947 and may well continue to expand with the influx of Catholic immigrants from Spanish-speaking and third world countries.

The percentage of American Jews (2%) has been decreasing since mid-century, due in part to a lower birth rate and a growing trend toward intermarriage. Mormons or Latter-day Saints, systematic evangelists, now make up 2% of the national population. Orthodox Church preference remains at less than 1%, while 2% give a preference for another church or religion.

The proportion with no religious preference at 10% has been increasing gradually since 1967.

It is important to bear in mind that this audit reports *preference* and not *membership*.

SIXTY-FIVE PERCENT CLAIM CHURCH OR SYNAGOGUE MEMBERSHIP

Question:
Do you happen to be a member of a church or synagogue?

NATIONAL	65 %
Men	58
Women	71
18-29 years	55
30-49 years	65
50 and older	73
East	64
Midwest	68
South	71
West	53
College graduates	64
College incomplete	66
High school graduates	68
Not H.S. graduates	60
Whites	65
Blacks	66
Hispanics	56
Protestants	72
Evangelicals	87
Non-evangelicals	59
Catholics	72

Findings are based on personal and telephone interviews with 4,597 adults nationwide during 1988.

Source: Gallup Poll

In 1988 a 65% majority of American adults claimed church or synagogue membership, down from 69% in 1987 and at present, the lowest membership figure recorded in Gallup survey history.

As in past years, however, women are more likely to be members than men (71% to 58%). Membership increases progressively with age, from 55% of young adults 18-29, to 73% of persons 50 and older. By region, more Southerners (71%) join churches than their counterparts in other parts of the country. Among education groups, high school graduates are most likely to report membership (68%), with college graduates at 64%.

The 1988 membership figure for whites (65%) is statistically the same as recorded in 1986 (68%). But notable declines are found among minority groups, with downtrends among blacks from 75% in 1986 to 66% in 1988, and among Hispanics from 68% in 1986 to 56% in 1988.

Protestants and Catholics affiliate in equal numbers (72%), closing the gap found two years earlier (72% to 81%), and indicating a significant drop in Catholic Church membership. Never before has the figure on Catholic membership matched that of Protestants. Evangelicals (87%) and Non-evangelicals (59%), however, differ widely on this measure.

Importantly, membership figures reported here are self-classified and thus may include some who are not actually on the rolls of a local church or synagogue. It should be noted also that adherents of certain churches — for example, the Roman Catholic and Eastern Orthodox — are considered members at birth.

FOUR IN TEN AMERICANS ATTEND RELIGIOUS SERVICES

Question:
Did you, yourself, happen to attend church or synagogue in the last seven days?

NATIONAL	42 %
Men	38
Women	46
18-29 years	33
30-49 years	41
50 and older	49
East	37
Midwest	48
South	45
West	36
College graduates	47
College incomplete	43
High school graduates	41
Not H.S. graduates	39
Whites	41
Blacks	47
Hispanics	41
Protestants	45
Evangelicals	60
Non-evangelicals	34
Catholics	48

Findings are based on personal and telephone interviews with 2,041 adults nationwide during 1988.

Source: Gallup Poll

During a typical week in 1988 four adults in every ten (42%) attended church or synagogue, with Protestants and Catholics attending in roughly equal numbers (45% to 48%), and a significant gap between Evangelicals (60%) and Non-evangelicals (34%).

Levels of churchgoing are higher among women than men by a margin of 46% to 38%, whereas blacks (47%) attend more frequently than whites (41%) Hispanics (41%).

Likelihood of attendance increases with age and education. Nearly half the population 50 or older (49%) reports attendance, compared to persons 30 to 49 (41%) and those 18 to 29 (33%). College graduates (47%) are more inclined than their counterparts to be churchgoers.

By region, attendance is highest among Southerners (45%), compared to Easterners (37%), the least likely among regional groups to attend church or synagogue.

OVER HALF OF U.S. TEENS ATTEND SERVICES

Questions:
Did you attend religious services in a church or synagogue during the last seven days?
What is your religious preference—Protestant, Roman Catholic, Jewish, or other?

	Protestant %	Catholic %	Attended church last week %
NATIONAL*	52	30	52
Male	51	30	49
Female	54	29	54
13 - 15 years	51	32	56
16 - 17 years	54	26	46
Whites	50	32	49
Blacks	77	8	68
White-collar family background	50	32	56
Blue-collar family background	54	27	48
East	41	43	46
Midwest	49	34	51
South	72	17	62
West	41	28	45
Central cities	48	36	49
Suburbs	45	31	52
Non-metropolitan	49	26	53

*The sample of Jewish teens was too small to provide projectible data.

Findings are based on nationwide telephone interviews with 1,518 teens 13 to 17 during March, June and August through October of 1987.

Source: Gallup Youth Survey

For most American teens the activities of a typical weekend include attending religious services, with more than half (52%) reporting they attended church or synagogue within the past week. Attendance is higher in the Bible Belt — the South (62%) and Midwest (51%) — than in the East (46%) and West (45%).

Black teens are more likely to attend than whites by a considerable margin of 68% to 49%, and young women more so than young men by 54% to 49%. Teens from white-collar households go to church more frequently than those from blue-collar families by 56% to 48%.

As teens grow older they are less likely to attend services. Among those 13 to 15, more than half (56%) say they went to church or synagogue in the last week. But for those 16 or older, attendance drops to less than half (46%).

Teens are more likely to give a Protestant than Catholic preference by 52% to 30%. The ratio of Protestants to Catholics is closer, however, among teens than adults. Only 7% of teens say they have no religious preference.

Although teens generally attend services more frequently than adults, it should be remembered that parents may require them to do so.

GAP BETWEEN 'BELIEVING' AND 'BELONGING' PERSISTS

Question:
Do you think a person can be a good Christian or Jew if he or she doesn't attend church or synagogue?

	Yes %	No %	No Opinion %
NATIONAL	76	20	4
Men	75	21	4
Women	78	19	3
18-24 years	77	19	4
25-29 years	84	12	4
30-49 years	79	18	3
50 and older	71	26	3
Whites	78	19	3
Blacks	68	28	4
Hispanics	64	31	5
East	77	19	4
Midwest	81	17	2
South	68	27	5
West	83	14	3
Protestants	72	25	3
Catholics	83	13	4
Other	81	16	3

By Decade

	Yes %	No %	No Opinion %
1988	76	20	4
1978	78	17	5
1964	67	25	8
1957	78	17	5

Findings are based on personal interviews with 2,556 adults nationwide during March 1988.

Source: Gallup Survey for the National Catholic Evangelization Association

Relatively few Americans believe church or synagogue attendance affects the quality of one's religious identity. Seventy-six percent nationwide think "a person can be a good Christian or Jew" apart from an organized religious community, a belief more prevalent among young adults 25 to 29 years old (84%), whites (78%) and Westerners (83%). Majorities of religious groups share this view, with Catholics, required by doctrine to attend mass, more likely than Protestants to agree by a margin of 83% to 2%.

The findings reveal the extent to which religious belief and practice may evolve in isolation from authoritative bodies: what many observers call the privatization of faith, and attribute largely to an ethos rooted firmly in the American tradition of religious freedom as a private matter of individual choice.

Even in 1957, when church and synagogue attendance reached one of its highest levels (47%), the majority of Americans (78%) separated religious group affiliation from identity with a faith. A later 1964 survey was taken on the eve of the cultural revolution, when disaffection from religious institutions was growing more pronounced. During that year the proportion that answered affirmatively dipped to 67%; an indication that more Americans were seeking the viability of traditional religious communities while facing the decade's social upheavals. Figures recorded in 1978 (78%) and 1988 (76%) match that in 1957, suggesting a pervasive religious privacy more related to social stability than attendance levels.

FOUR IN TEN REPORT EXTENDED ABSENCE FROM CHURCH OR SYNAGOGUE

Question:
Has there ever been a period of two years or more when you did not attend church or synagogue, apart from weddings, funerals, or special holidays such as Christmas, Easter, or Yom Kippur?

	Yes %	No %	Don't know %
NATIONAL	42	57	1
Men	46	52	2
Women	38	61	1
18-24 years	33	67	*
25-29 years	44	55	1
30-49 years	47	52	1
50 and older	39	60	1
Whites	43	56	1
Blacks	34	64	2
Hispanics	27	72	1
Protestants	41	58	1
Catholics	35	64	1
Other	45	53	2

*Less than one percent.

Findings are based on personal interviews with 2,556 adults nationwide during March 1988.

Source: Gallup Survey for the National Catholic Evangelization Association

our in ten Americans (42%) say that at some time in their lives they have stopped ttending church or synagogue for a period of two years or more. This is more the case or men than women by a margin of 46% to 38%.

'ersons in their thirties and forties report the highest incidence of extended absence 17%), far more than those 18 to 24 (33%), but roughly the same proportion as adults 5 to 29 (44%). Far fewer respondents 50 and older (39%) did not attend for two years r more, indicating a notable generation gap in behaviors and attitudes toward ngoing religious affiliation.

Vith traditional ties to Catholicism, Hispanics (27%) are least inclined to leave the hurch for prolonged periods, compared to blacks (34%) and whites (43%), far more kely to be unchurched.

'hirty-five percent of Catholics have left the church for two years or more, with 'rotestants at 41% and persons with other religious preferences at 45%.

Vhen asked why they stopped attending church or synagogue, respondents most ften cited other activities (26%), increased independence of choice (25%), relocation 22%) and specific problems with or objections to the church, its teaching or members 20%). At least one in ten respondents said that their lifestyles had become incompat- ole with religious participation (13%), that the church no longer helped them find neaning or purpose (13%), or that work schedules conflicted with going to church or emple (12%).

ORGANIZED RELIGION TAKES ITS TEST

Question:
Would you tell me after each [statement] whether you strongly agree, are uncertai moderately disagree, or strongly disagree?

	Strongly agree %	Moderately agree %	Uncertain %	Strongly disagree %	Don kno %
Most churches and synagogues today have a clear sense of the real spiritual nature of religion.	48	32	8	8	4
The rules about morality preached by the churches and synagogues today are too restrictive.	9	23	22	28	18
Most churches and synagogues today are warm and accepting of outsiders.	24	40	19	12	5
Most churches and synagogues today are too concerned with organizational, as opposed to theological or spiritual issues.	24	35	25	13	3
Most churches and synagogues today are not concerned enough with social justice.	14	27	30	22	7
Most churches and synagogues today are effective in helping people find meaning in life.	22	45	18	11	4

Findings are based on personal interviews with 2,556 adults nationwide during March 198

Source: Gallup Survey for the National Catholic Evangelization Association

Eight in ten Americans (80%) feel that most churches and synagogues have a clear sense of the spiritual dimension of religious life, with 48% who agree strongly and 32% moderately.

A less pronounced consensus is found on the extent to which organized religion is effectively helping people find meaning.Twenty-two percent agree strongly on the issue, against 45% who agree moderately and 18% uncertain. The relative ambivalence reflects the staggering diversity of religious beliefs and practices in this country, which complicates the pursuit of purpose and meaning among Americans.

Concerning morality or ethics, opinion is evenly distributed among numbers who agree moderately (23%), are uncertain (22%), or strongly disagree (28%) that rules of conduct being preached are too restrictive. Only 9% agree strongly. The total percentage in agreement at 32% is up from 27% recorded in 1978.

An uptrend occurred also among those who say religious bodies are too concerned with organizational matters, from 51% in 1978 to 59% in 1988. The increases on organizational issues and restrictive preaching are greater among churched than unchurched respondents.

A 64% majority feels that most churches and synagogues accept "outsiders," but those on the outside, the unchurched, agree far less than churchgoers by a margin of 53% to 73%. Blacks are slightly more likely than whites to agree by 69% to 66%.

The percentage saying that clergy and congregations are not enough concerned with social justice has increased since 1978 from 35% to 41%, which suggests a lesser regard for the role of organized religion in redressing the inequalities of privilege and poverty in America today.

CHURCHGOING UNCHANGED BY RELIGIOUS TV

Questions:
Has watching religious TV changed your involvement in your local church or synagogue? Has your involvement increased or decreased?

(Based on total viewers)

Has not changed involvement			90 %
Has changed involvement			8
	Increased	4	
	Decreased	2	
	Not sure	2	
Not sure			2
			100 %

Question:
By any chance, have you contributed money to any television evangelists in the last twelve months?

Have contributed			4 %
Total viewers			8
	Within past 7 days	12	
	Within past 8-30 days	4	
	31 days or more	3	
Non-viewers			*

*Less than one percent.

Findings are based on personal interviews with 1,571 adults nationwide during April 1987.

Source: Gallup Poll

This survey refutes one of the principal criticisms of the TV ministries — that they tend to dissipate viewers' interest in their local churches. Nine viewers in ten said that watching religious TV has not affected their involvement. Those saying their participation has changed are more likely to cite more rather than less local church activity.

Four percent of the total sample — roughly seven million adults — said they had contributed money to one or more TV evangelists within the last 12 months. The proportion of donors rises to 8% among all religious TV viewers, and to 12% among weekly viewers.

Roughly half of all contributors reported donations of less than $100 to TV evangelists during the last year, and half said they gave more than $100.

A majority of donors said they did not expect to change the amount of their contributions during the next twelve months, while about one-fifth said they planned to give more. A similar proportion said they probably would give less.

CHURCHES RARELY CALLED RACIST

Question:
Have you ever felt unwelcome or excluded from any church because of your race or ethnicity?

	Yes %	No %	Don't know %
NATIONAL	4	95	1
Whites	3	96	1
Blacks	8	92	*
Hispanics	3	95	2
East	3	95	2
Midwest	3	96	1
South	4	95	1
West	6	92	2
Protestants	4	95	1
Catholics	3	96	1
Other	9	90	1
Churched	4	95	1
Unchurched	4	94	2

*Less than one percent.

Findings are based on personal interviews with 2,556 adults nationwide during March 1988.

Source: Gallup Survey for the National Catholic Evangelization Association

If culturally diverse as a whole, churches in America are known to be largely homogeneous; hence the infrequency of reports of exclusion from churches due to race or ethnicity (4%). As the target group of institutional racism in the U.S., however, blacks (8%) are more likely to cite exclusion than Hispanics and whites (3% each). Among churchgoing blacks, the percentage rises to 10%, compared to 5% of unchurched blacks. The difference is much less pronounced among whites and Hispanics in the same categories.

Regionally, Westerners (6%) report racial or ethnic exclusion most often, which may account in some measure for related findings that suggest higher levels of church disaffection in the West.

Few Protestants (4%) and Catholics (3%) report discrimination in the church, although the numbers rise among those with other religious preferences (9%). Churched and unchurched respondents indicate no difference in proportions responding affirmatively (4%).

HOMOSEXUALS IN CLERGY GAINING ACCEPTANCE

Question:
Do you think homosexuals should or should not be hired for . . .

The Clergy

	1987 %	1985 %	1977 %
Yes	42	41	36

	1987 %	1985 %	1977 %
No	51	53	54

	1987 %	1985 %	1977 %
No opinion	6	6	10

Latest findings are based on telephone interviews with 1,015 adults nationwide during March 1987.

Source: Gallup Poll

Although actions and statements against homosexuality have been undertaken by several religious groups, results from recent Gallup surveys reveal growing acceptance of homosexuals in the ranks of clergy by the general public.

In 1977 36% nationwide said that homosexuals should be welcomed as members of the clergy. Since then, the figure has slowly climbed to a new high of 42% in 1987.

Half the population (51%) in 1987 opposed homosexuals in the clergy, a proportion that declined slightly from 54% in 1977. The percentage with no opinion dropped four points, from 10% to 6% in 1987.

CATHOLICS ASSESS THEIR CHURCH

Question:
What kind of job do you think the Catholic Church in the United States is doing in handling the following—excellent, good, only fair or poor? ("Excellent" and "good" ratings comprise positive assessments; "only fair" and "poor" comprise the negative.)

Serving needs of:	Positive %	Negative %	No opinion %
Families	58	39	3
The elderly	54	42	4
Yourself	50	46	4
Minorities	41	49	10
New immigrants	38	47	15
Single people	30	62	8
Separated, divorced, remarried Catholics	30	63	7

Church Practices/Policies

	Positive %	Negative %	No opinion %
Church's relations with non-Christians	54	38	8
Role of lay people	52	41	7
Changes since 2nd Vatican Council	47	46	7
Role of women	37	60	3
Involvement in politics and public policy	27	63	10
Marriage annulment system	26	60	14

Findings are based on telephone interviews with 239 Roman Catholics, out of a total sample of 1,004 adults nationwide during March 1986.

Source: Gallup Survey for *The People's Religion*, George Gallup, Jr. and Jim Castelli (New York: Macmillan Publishing Co., Inc.), in press.

U.S. Catholics give their church high marks for relations with non-Christians and for handling the role of the laity; for example, by creating greater participation on the part of rank-and-file membership.

Opinion is divided more closely on the sweeping changes since the Second Vatican Council, which under Pope John XXIII modernized all aspects of church life and eliminated the Latin mass.

On the Church's involvement in politics, public policy, the role of women and marriage annulment, Catholics show signs of discontent, and majorities give a negative assessment.

When asked to rate the Church on serving needs of seven key population groups, Catholics most highly ranked service to families and the elderly. Ministry to the individual and minorities received mixed opinion, while works on behalf of new immigrants, singles, separated, divorced and remarried Catholics ranked least.

CATHOLIC MAJORITY FAVORS ORDAINING WOMEN

Question:
Please tell me how much you agree or disagree with this statement:

It would be a good thing if women were allowed to be ordained as priests.

(Views of Catholics)

	National Opinion Research Center	Gallup Surveys			*NY Times*/CBS News Poll
	1974 %	1977 %	1979 %	1982 %	1985 %
NATIONAL					
Agree	29	36	40	44	52
Disagree	65	57	53	50	35
No opinion	6	7	7	6	13

Latest Gallup findings are based on personal interviews with 1,323 self-identified Catholics of a total of 4,592 adults nationwide during May and June 1982.

Source: Gallup Survey for the Quixote Center and Priests for Equality

Support among Catholics for ordination of women as priests has steadily increased since 1974. A 52% majority favors women in the clergy against 35% who oppose, according to a *New York Times*/CBS News Poll conducted in 1985. That year 13% of Catholics expressed no opinion.

The 1985 poll showed that American adults nationwide favor women's ordination by 47% to 28% who oppose. Non-Catholics support women in the clergy by a margin of 45% to 25%.

In the latest Gallup survey of 1982 a total of 44% of Catholics expressed either strong or moderate support, while a combined total of 50% opposed. Comparison with figures from 1974, with 29% favoring and 65% opposing, reveal the increased measure of support for women in the Catholic clergy.

Men More Likely to Favor Change

Ironically, Catholic men are more likely than women to favor women in the priesthood by 50% to 39%.

In addition younger Catholics, the college-educated and those in higher income brackets are more likely to favor women's ordination.

Catholics Favoring Ordination of Women

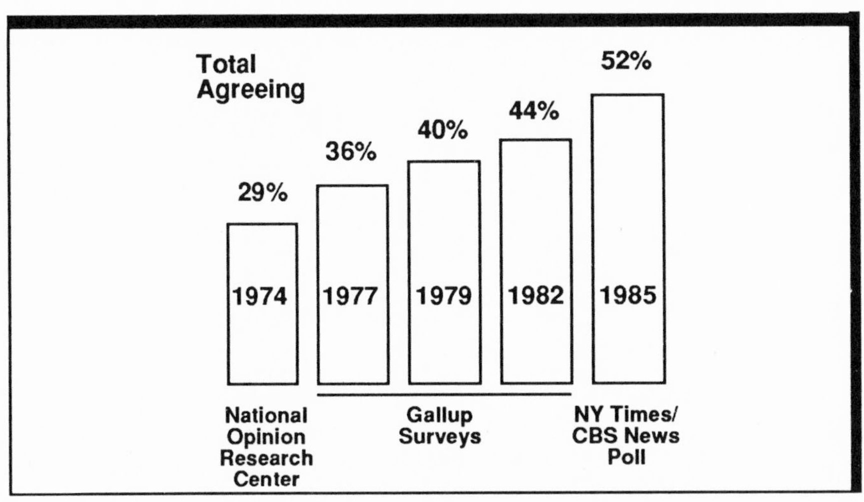

POPE'S POPULARITY WANES

Question:
Using this card, with the highest position of plus five indicating a person you have a very favorable opinion of, and the lowest position of minus five indicating a person you have a very unfavorable opinion of — how far up the scale or how far down the scale would you rate Pope John Paul II?

(Plus 5, plus 4 ratings)

	NATIONAL %	Catholic %	Protestant %
1987	48	69	40
1984	55	82	48
1982	54	80	46
1981 (Assasination attempt)	65	83	60
1980	59	85	51
1979	56	80	47

By comparison, the "highly favorable" ratings given previous Popes:

	NATIONAL %	Catholic %	Protestant %
Pope Paul VI *(1963-1978)*			
1977	37	66	26
1976	25	48	19
Pope John XXII *(1958-1963)*			
1960	32	76	16

Latest findings are based on interviews with 1,607 adults nationwide during July 1987.

Source: Gallup Poll

A plurality of Americans (48%) gave Pope John Paul II a "highly favorable" rating prior to his trip to the United States in 1987, but opinion has dropped in recent years on the heels of statements limiting the role of women and censoring some U.S. Catholic theologians. These are among the reasons for discontent within the Church, according to related surveys measuring satisfaction with Roman polity.

The Pope's rating is based on the top two positions (plus 5 and plus 4) on a 10-point attitude scale which measures intensity of feeling, both positive and negative.

Figures show the trend in John Paul's ratings since 1979, when his tour of this country clearly boosted public opinion to levels he sustained in subsequent measurements into 1981. The upturn in that year may partly reflect sympathy for him following the attempt on his life.

Among American Catholics regard for the Pope has declined sharply since 1984, while Protestant opinion has followed a general downtrend since 1981.

OF FOURTEEN NATIONS AMERICANS ARE MOST SATISFIED WITH THEIR CHURCH

Question:
Generally speaking, do you think that your church is giving, in your country, adequate answers to . . . man's spiritual needs?

	Yes %	No %	Don't know %
United States	73	14	13
Republic of Ireland	64	24	12
Northern Ireland	60	24	15
Finland	58	21	21
Norway	50	28	22
France	48	37	15
West Germany	47	33	20
Spain	45	37	18
Italy	43	29	28
Great Britain	42	32	26
Belgium	40	29	31
Sweden	37	35	29
Netherlands	33	29	38
Denmark	26	45	29

Note: Results do not add to 100% due to rounding or no response.

Findings are based on a survey conducted in fourteen nations during 1981.

Source: Gallup International Research Institutes (GIRI) for the Center for Applied Research in the Apostolate (CARA) and the European Value System Study Group

Three in every four Americans (73%) hold the view that the church in the U.S. is providing adequate answers to spiritual needs. According to an international Gallup Poll, the American public expresses more satisfaction on this question than persons of all fourteen nations surveyed.

Least likely to say the church is meeting spiritual needs are the Swedish, Dutch and Danish. Conversely, citizens of the Republic of Ireland respond more affirmatively than respondents in all nations except the U.S. Though torn by religious strife and terrorism, the Northern Irish follow third.

Italians on the other hand, who share Vatican soil, rank ninth among those who agree the church adequately answers the needs of the human spirit.

IV. Ethics and Values

Sixty-three percent of American adults have expressed discontent with the nation's moral climate, particularly dishonesty in public life. Before the 1988 presidential election 79% said that honesty would be more important an issue than in past elections, while in a separate survey that year, only 16% favorably rated the ethical standards of congressional officials. Although regard is higher for the ethics of clergy, the drop from 67% in 1985 to 60% in 1988 suggests the scandals surrounding some TV evangelists have shaken public confidence in the viability of church leadership.

Americans may value civic virtue, but they disagree on principles for determining a moral basis. Forty-three percent think morality should stem from traditional religious values, about the same percentage (44%) saying ethics should reflect the history of human experience.

Nonetheless, an overwhelming majority of eight in ten (79%) said in 1988 that "clear guidelines about what's good and evil apply to everyone regardless of the situation," a possible signal of the ebb of moral relativism in this country. Perceptions differ, though, on the rigidity of ethical guidelines. Thirty-eight percent agreed "completely" with the statement, while 41% agreed "mostly" and thus believe there can be rare exceptions to such guidelines.

In 1986 over half of U. S. adults (52%) described their values as "moderate," compared to 36% with "traditional" or conservative values, and 11% "liberal." But in the private realm of family and marriage, the proportion claiming traditional values shot up to 85% in 1988. Importantly, 66% of that sample disagreed that "women should return to their traditional role in society," an indication that Americans are revising the traditional family ethic to meet the economic and ethical demands of equal opportunity for women. Another 1988 survey, however, showed that nearly all Americans (95%) would welcome "more emphasis on traditional family ties."

Related findings verify a resurgence of conservative morality in the U. S. Only 39% in 1985 called premarital sex wrong, a percentage that had steadily declined since the 1960s. In 1987 that proportion rose to 46%, a significant reversal of a twenty-year trend that reflects growing anxiety about AIDS and sexually transmitted disease. On the more divisive issue of abortion, public opinion remains unchanged, with a 57% majority favoring legal abortions under certain circumstances.

Americans want a more ethical society, but they disagree on how to create it. Forty-three percent in 1987 supported teaching ethics in public schools, while 36% said moral instruction should be left to parents and churches. There is no consensus on treating the drug epidemic, which respondents in 1988 cited as the nation's greatest dilemma. Forty-seven percent favor educating youth about drugs, and 35% advise keeping drugs out of the country. If divided over personal and private morality, moreover, Americans are calling for a moral reformation of the public sector.

AMERICANS IDENTIFY VALUES

Question:
Some people have very traditional values about such matters as sex,morality, family life and religion. If 1 represents someone who has very traditional, old-fashioned values and 7 represents someone who has very liberal modern values about these matters, where on this scale would you place yourself?

	Traditional (1's, 2's) %	Moderate (3's, 4's, 5's) %	Liberal (6's, 7's) %
NATIONAL	36	52	11
Democrats	40	51	8
Republicans	38	53	9
Protestants	41	51	7
Catholics	29	56	14
Whites	37	52	10
Blacks	35	50	15
Men	31	54	14
Women	41	49	9
18-29 years	20	58	21
30-49 years	33	55	11
50 and older	52	43	4
College grads.	27	62	11
College inc.	30	58	12
High school grads.	34	53	12
Not H.S. grads.	54	35	10
Political philosophy:			
Left of center	32	53	15
Middle of road	31	58	10
Right of center	45	46	9
East	31	58	10
Midwest	33	55	11
South	45	43	11
West	34	53	13

Note: "No opinion," 1% nationally, omitted.

Findings are based on personal interviews with 1,552 adults nationwide during April 1986.

Source: Gallup Poll

On values relating to sex, morality, family life and religion, the views of most Americans range between extremely conservative and extremely liberal, although the weight of opinion is decidedly conservative.

About half of survey respondents (52%) place themselves in moderate positions on a seven-point scale designed to measure social values, while 36% take positions on the right and 11% on the left.

The survey suggests that the Democratic and Republican parties seeking to win votes on social issues with a strong moral content start with about an even advantage: 38% of Republicans place themselves on the traditional side, 53% in moderate positions, and 9% on the liberal side. These figures almost exactly match those for Democrats: 40%, 51%, and 8% respectively.

Protestants More Likely to Lean to Right

Neither strongly liberal nor strongly conservative, the college educated by three in five (62%) opt for moderate points on the scale. However, traditional values outweigh the liberal in this group by a 27% to 11% margin. Persons whose formal education ended before high school graduation come down strongly in favor of traditional values, by 54% to 10%.

The survey also shows women, older persons and Southerners to be more traditionally oriented than their opposite numbers.

Those indicating a political philosophy right of center are somewhat more inclined than others to place themselves on the traditional side of the values scale, but the overall differences on the two scales are not as pronounced as might be expected.

Protestants (41%) are considerably more likely to lean to the right on the values scale than Catholics (29%). Little difference is found between whites and blacks, with 37% of whites and 35% of blacks placing themselves on the traditional side of the scale.

U.S. PUBLIC APPRAISES MORAL FOUNDATIONS

Question:
Should morality and ethics be based more on traditional religious values, or more on man's experience over the centuries?

Traditional religious values	43 %
Man's experience over the centuries	44
Both (volunteered)	9
No opinion	4
	100 %

Question:
In your opinion, which is more responsible for the advancement of mankind—traditional religious values, or man's reason and intellect, based on his learning experience?

Traditional religious values	40 %
Man's reason and intellect	49
Both (volunteered)	7
No opinion	4
	100 %

Findings are based on telephone interviews with 511 adults nationwide during May 1987.

Source: Gallup Survey for the Christian Broadcasting Network, Inc.

Large numbers of Americans who belong to churches and believe in God depend on human reason and experience to resolve difficulties and shape values, according to a recent Gallup survey.

Results indicate the degree to which many place faith in human resources ahead of reliance on higher powers such as God.

Religious Values Versus Reason

Asked whether "traditional religious values" or "man's reason and intellect" was more responsible for "the advancement of mankind," nearly half, 49%, chose reason and intellect, while 40% credited religious values and seven percent said "both."

Those most likely to attribute progress to reason and intellect were young people from 18 to 29 (58%), college graduates (61%) and Non- evangelicals (56%). In addition high school graduates (47%) and Evangelicals (56%) gave more credit to religious values.

Responses split evenly on the question of whether morals and ethics should be based more on "religious values" or "human experiences over the centuries." Forty-four percent chose experience and 43% religious values.

Far more Evangelicals (56%) than Non-evangelicals (34%) draw on religious values for moral guidelines. Conversely, 48% of Non-evangelicals look to human experience, compared to 35% of the Evangelicals.

TRADITIONAL SOCIAL VALUES GAIN BROADER PUBLIC SUPPORT

Question:
Here are some social changes which might occur in coming years. Would you welcome these or not welcome them? *More emphasis on self-expression? Less emphasis on money? More acceptance of sexual freedom? More emphasis on traditional family ties? More respect for authority? Less emphasis on working hard? More acceptance of marijuana usage?*

	Welcome %	Not welcome %	No opinion %
More family ties			
1988	94	3	3
1981	92	5	3
1978	91	5	4
More respect for authority			
1988	89	7	4
1981	89	6	5
1978	89	6	5
More self-expression*			
1988	73	14	13
1978	75	15	10
Less money emphasis			
1988	67	23	10
1981	71	21	8
1978	70	21	9
Less work emphasis			
1988	24	70	6
1981	28	66	6
1978	25	69	6
More sexual freedom			
1988	22	68	10
1981	25	67	8
1978	29	62	9
More marijuana acceptance			
1988	8	87	5
1981	13	82	5
1978	20	74	6

*Not asked in 1981.

Latest findings are based on personal interviews of 2,556 adults nationwide during March 1988.

Source: Gallup Survey for the National Catholic Evangelization Association.

Most Americans cling to traditional social values and would welcome stronger family ties, greater respect for authority, more emphasis on hard work, and less on money. At the same time demands for greater sexual freedom and tolerance of marijuana have softened over the last ten years, especially among young adults.

A 1988 Gallup survey found virtually unanimous public support for increased emphasis on traditional family values (94%) and respect for authority (89%). Large majorities also favor greater opportunity for self-expression (73%) and a less emphasis on money (67%), while 70% would welcome more emphasis on working hard.

Conservative social values have retained as much public appeal as in 1981 and 1987, when similar majorities indicted they would welcome added emphasis on these values.

However, substantial trends are apparent in attitudes toward sexual freedom and marijuana usage: in both cases, current attitudes are more conservative than a decade ago. Particularly dramatic is the increased rejection of drugs, especially among young adults. General public tolerance of marijuana dropped from 20% in 1978 to 8% in 1988, with those 18 to 29 who accept marijuana down from 74% in 1978 to 87% in 1988.

The same period witnessed a gradual decline in public demand for sexual freedom, from 29% in 1978 to 25% in 1981 and 22% in 1988 — doubtless because of the AIDS epidemic. Again, the most dramatic shifts on this issue occurred among young adults, nonetheless more likely to favor sexual freedom (35%) than 30 to 49 year olds (22%) or persons 50 and older (13%).

TRADITIONAL VALUES INCLUDE EQUALITY

Question:
Please tell me how much you agree or disagree with each of these statements.

	Completely agree %	Mostly agree %	Mostly disagree %	Completely disagree %	No opinion %
I have old-fashioned values about family and marriage.	50	35	9	4	2
	85		13		
Women should return to their traditional role in society.	11	20	30	36	3
	31		36		
We have gone too far in pushing equal rights in this country.	16	28	32	20	4
	44		52		

Findings are based on personal interviews with 3,021 adults nationwide during May 1988.

Source: Gallup Survey for *Times Mirror*

Despite the staggering divorce rate in America, 85% of U.S. adults claim to have traditional family values. The traditional family ethic holds slightly more among women (86%) than men (84%), but considerably more for those over 50 (94%) than persons under 30 (77%) and between 30 and 49 (83%). About as many Protestants (84%) as Catholics (86%)have conservative values, though levels of agreement range among Evangelicals (96%), Non-evangelicals (83%), white Protestants (92%) and black Protestants (76%).

A 66% majority opposes women's return to traditional roles: an indication that Americans are redefining time-honored social arrangements to accommodate a more complex experience of marriage as well as the values that shape the family. The number of working married women with children has shot up from 30% in 1970 to 57% in 1987, and adults are adjusting their values to the reality of women in the labor force.

Sixty-seven percent of females disagree that women should resume traditional roles, an opinion shared equally by males (65%). Majorities of Catholics (65%), Jews (65%) and Protestants (66%) hold this view, with white Protestants at 65% and black Protestants at 68%. Fifty-eight percent of Evangelicals and 70% of Non-evangelicals would not support women's return to traditional social roles.

Alhough 44% of Americans think equal rights in this country have been overpromoted, a 52% majority disagrees. Women are more likely than men to disagree by 56% to 49%, with a more substantial margin of 76% to 49% between blacks and whites. Protestants are evenly divided with 47% agreeing and 50% disagreeing, but striking differences are found by race among Protestants. Fifty-one percent of white Protestants feel that equal rights have been pushed too far; 76%of black Protestants disagree. Evangelicals express more agreement than Non-evangelicals by 55% to 49%. Conversely, majorities of Catholics (51%) and Jews (64%) disagree.

FEWER HEED SITUATION ETHICS

Question:
Please tell me how much you agree or disagree with [this] statement.

There are clear guidelines about what's good or evil that apply to everyone regardless of their situation.

NATIONAL

Completely agree		Mostly agree		Mostly disagree		Completely disagree		Don't know	
1988	1987	1988	1987	1988	1987	1988	1987	1988	1987
38%	34%	41%	45%	12%	12%	6%	4%	4%	5%

Latest findings are based on personal interviews with 3,021 adults during May 1988.

Source: Gallup Survey for *Times Mirror*

Best-selling scholar Alan Bloom argues in *The Closing of the American Mind* that a "new language of value relativism" has effectively prevented Americans from talking with any conviction about good and evil. Nonetheless, recent Gallup findings indicate that most Americans feel absolute guidelines determining good and evil apply to all regardless of the circumstances.

In 1988, on the heels of moral crises in federal government, on Wall Street and among some TV evangelists, nearly eight in ten (79%) agreed "completely" or "mostly" to there being "clear guidelines about what's good and evil" with universal application. The proportion in strong agreement increased from 34% to 38% during a year when Americans scrutinized public and private morality in earnest. The findings suggest relativistic values may not be as widespread as the ethical ambiguities that beset American life.

Men and women agree on a universal morality in roughly the same numbers, by 78% to 79%. Hispanics (82%) are slightly more inclined to do so than whites (79%) and blacks (80%). Eighty-four percent of all Protestants favor ethical absolutes, with white Protestants at 84% and black Protestants at 81%, compared to 90% of Evangelicals and 80% of Non-evangelicals. Fewer Catholics (75%) and Jews (66%) agree to such standards.

AMERICANS DISSASTISFIED WITH NATION'S MORAL CLIMATE

Question:
On the whole, would you say you are satisfied or dissatisfied with the honesty and standards of behavior of people in this country today?

	Satisfied %	Dissatisfied %	No opinion %
NATIONAL	33	63	4
Men	35	61	4
Women	30	65	5
Whites	34	62	4
Blacks	21	73	6
18-29 years	36	60	4
30-49 years	36	60	4
50 and older	26	70	4
College grads.	43	55	2
College inc.	32	64	4
High school grads.	31	64	5
Non H.S. grads.	27	68	5
Family income:			
$25,000 and over	39	59	2
Under $25,000	29	66	5
Moral values:			
Traditional	26	69	5
Moderate	37	60	3
Liberal	33	64	3

Here is the trend:

	Satisfied %	Dissatisfied %	No opinion %
1986	33	63	4
1973	22	72	6
1963	34	58	8

Latest findings are based on personal interviews with 1,552 adults nationwide during April 1986.

Source: Gallup Poll

Amid widespread recent reports of unethical and illegal activities in many areas of public life, almost two-thirds of Americans express dissatisfaction with the honesty and standards of behavior of their compatriots.

In the latest Gallup assessment 63% say that on the whole they are dissatisfied with the honesty of people in this country, while about half of that proportion, 33%, are satisfied.

The current findings reflect those recorded in the first Gallup measurement in 1963, but represent a modest improvement over the results of a Gallup Poll taken at the height of the Watergate affair in 1973. In that survey dissatisfaction outweighed satisfaction by better than a 3-to-1 ratio, 72% to 22%.

Although majorities in all major population groups show discontent with the current ethical climate in the U.S., somewhat greater concern appears among blacks, persons 50 and older, the less affluent, the less educated, and persons who share traditional moral values. Differences by gender are too small to be meaningful.

HONESTY IN GOVERNMENT CONCERNS ELECTORATE

Question:
In this year's presidential election, do you feel the issue of honesty in government is likely to be more important or less important than in previous elections?

	More important %	About the same (vol.) %	Less important %	No opinion %
NATIONAL	79	7	12	2
Republicans	77	7	12	4
Democrats	83	7	9	1
Independents	79	6	14	1

Question:
Some former Reagan Administration officials [were] accused of unlawful or unethical conduct. Is it your impression that the Reagan Administration's overall record for honesty and ethical standards is better or worse than most other recent administrations?

	Better than others %	Same (vol.) %	Worse than others %	No opinion %
NATIONAL	31	24	41	4
Republicans	54	25	17	4
Democrats	12	20	62	6
Independents	28	26	43	3

Findings are based on telephone interviews with 613 adults nationwide during February 1988

Source: Gallup Poll

Nearly eight in ten (79%) Americans in 1988 said the issue of honesty in government would weigh more heavily in their choice of a president than it had in previous elections.

Prior to the poll several past and present Reagan Administration officials had been charged with unlawful or unethical conduct, resulting in some highly publicized legal proceedings and Congressional hearings.

The overwhelming level of public concern over what was called the "sleaze factor" cut across political lines, with Democrats (83%) only slightly more likely than Republicans (77%) to place more emphasis on honesty. Overall 12% said the issue would be less important and 7% about the same.

Four in ten (41%) believed the Reagan Administration's record for honesty and ethical standards was worse than those compiled under most other recent presidents, while about a third (31%) rated Reagan's record better than others and 24% the same.

As might be expected Republicans (54%) were far more inclined than Democrats (12%) to consider the Reagan record better than average. But about one Republican in six (17%) considered it worse.

PROFESSIONAL ETHICS COME UNDER REVIEW

Question:
How would you rate the honesty and ethical standards of people in these different fields—very high, high, average, low or very low?

	Very high/high %
Druggists, pharmacists	66
Clergymen	60
College teachers	54
Medical doctors	53
Dentists	51
Engineers	48
Policemen	47
Bankers	26
Funeral directors	24
Journalists	23
TV reporters, commentators	22
Newspaper reporters	22
Building contractors	22
Senators	19
Lawyers	18
Business executives	16
Congressmen	16
Local office holders	14
Labor union leaders	14
Real estate agents	13
Stockbrokers	13
State office holders	11
Insurance salesmen	10
Advertising practitioners	7
Car salesmen	6

Findings are based on personal interviews with 1,030 adults nationwide during September 1988.

Source: Gallup Poll

Pharmacists and clergy are perceived by the public to have higher "honesty and ethical standards" than people employed in twenty-three other occupations.

Although some occupations receive low ratings in these studies, it is important to bear in mind that the findings reflect the public's perceptions and not necessarily the true ethical standards of the groups studied. Nevertheless, the results suggest a call for remedial efforts on the part of poorly rated professions and occupations.

Pharmacists Top List

For the first time since pharmacists have been included in the audit, they have topped the scale, with 66% giving them a very high or high ethical rating. Next are clergy, with a 60% positive rating.

From 1981 to 1985 the clergy slightly outranked pharmacists, though not by statistically significant margins. In 1985, for example, 67% gave the clergy a favorable grade, compared to 65% for pharmacists. In terms of "very high" ratings —the top position on the scale — the clergy continue to be more highly regarded than pharmacists, 22% to 14%.

The next highest rated occupations are college teachers, medical doctors, dentists, engineers and policemen, with overall positive scores ranging from 54% to 47%.

In the next tier are bankers, funeral directors, journalists, television reporters and commentators, newspaper reporters and building contractors, with favorable ratings from 26% to 22%.

Ten occupational groups are given very high or high ratings ranging from 19% to 10%. These are: senators, lawyers, business executives, congressional officials, local political officeholders, labor union leaders, real estate agents, stockbrokers, state political officeholders and insurance salesmen. Advertising practitioners and car salesmen occupy the last two positions, receiving positive ratings of 7% and 6%, respectively.

Collectively the occupations that receive the lowest scores for honesty and ethics are those that involve selling. Only about one person in ten rates the ethics of real estate agents, stockbrokers, insurance salesmen, advertising practitioners or car salesmen in positive terms. In contrast about four in ten rate each of these occupations as very low or low.

CHARACTER EDUCATION IN SCHOOLS WIDELY FAVORED

Question:
It has been proposed that the public schools include courses on 'character education' to help students develop personal values and ethical behavior. Do you think that courses on values and ethical behavior should be taught in the public schools, or do you think that this should be left to the students' parents and the churches?

	NATIONAL %	No children in school %	Public school parents %	Nonpublic school parents %
Yes, school	43	42	45	54
No, parents and churches	36	36	38	31
Both (volunteered)	13	13	13	11
Don't know	8	9	4	4

Question:
If courses about values and ethical behavior were required in the local public schools, who do you think should have the most to say about the content of the courses? The federal government in Washington, the state government, the local school board, the school administrators, the teachers, or the parents?

	NATIONAL %
Parents	42
Local school board	24
Teachers	14
School administrators	10
State government	9
Federal government	5
Don't know	12

Note: Figures add to more than 100% because of multiple responses.

Findings are based on personal interviews with 1,571 adults nationwide during April 1987.

Source: 19th Annual Gallup Poll/Phi Delta Kappa Survey.

America's ethical disarray has raised the question of early moral development and whose responsibility it is. When asked about character education, 43% of U.S. adults say that courses on values and ethical conduct should be taught in schools. Another 13% volunteer that schools, parents and churches together should take part in character education. Moreover, a total of 56% favor moral instruction in the classroom.

Content of Character Education Courses

In a related study six in ten Americans (62%) said that it would be possible to develop course contents on ethics and values which most community residents would find acceptable. About two in ten (23%) felt such contents could not be acceptably designed.

By a substantial margin Americans say that parents should most influence contents. Forty-two percent favor parental input, while 24% support school boards. Far fewer suggest teachers (14%) and administrators (10%), with state and federal governments at 9% and 5% respectively.

By a margin of almost five to three, respondents would favor excusing students from character education if their parents objected to subject matter.

SEX EDUCATION GAINS SUPPORT

Questions:
Do you feel the public elementary schools in this community should or should not teach sex education in grades four through eight?

(Those who responded affirmatively were asked:)
Should this program include discussions about AIDS, or not?

	Favor			Oppose	No opinion
		Discuss AIDS			
	Total	Yes	No		
	%	%	%	%	%
NATIONAL	71	67	4	21	8
Men	67	63	4	28	5
Women	74	70	4	16	10
18-29 years	80	74	6	16	4
30-49 years	78	75	3	17	5
50 and older	57	53	4	30	13
Attended college	81	77	4	15	4
No college	64	61	3	25	11

Findings are based on telephone interviews with 503 adults nationwide during February 1987.

Source: Gallup Poll

Americans' acceptance of sex education in their local elementary schools has risen sharply during the last two years, doubtless in response to the AIDS epidemic and the alarming increase in teenage pregnancies. In addition the vast majority of those favoring sex education for young children feel the curriculum should include discussion of AIDS.

In a 1987 Gallup Poll 71% expressed support for sex education classes in grades four through eight of their local public schools, while 21% opposed. As recently as 1985 approval outweighed disapproval by a narrow 52% to 43% margin. And in the Poll's first assessment in 1981, statistically equivalent numbers favored (45%) and opposed (48%) sex education in elementary schools.

As in past surveys women, younger adults of both sexes, and persons who attended college are more supportive than their opposite numbers. But majorities in all population groups now favor sex instruction for young children.

To a large extent AIDS has influenced public opinion on the general topic of sex education. Virtually all (upwards of 90%) in every group of those favoring elementary school classes on sex feel discussion about AIDS should be part of the curriculum.

TEENS EXAMINE VALUES

Question:
How important — very important, fairly important, or not so important — do you think it is for a person your age to learn each of the following personal qualities?

"Very Important"	**NATIONAL %**
Honesty	89
Responsibility	89
Self-respect	87
Hard work	70
Independence	65
Patience	61
Obedience	60
Religious faith	44

Findings are based on telephone interviews with 503 teens (13 to 17) nationwide during March 1987.

Source: Gallup Youth Survey

According to a 1987 Gallup Youth Survey, less than half of American teens (44%) say it is "very important" for people their age to develop religious faith. By comparison, 51% of teens in 1984 stressed the importance of personal faith development: a downtrend observers attribute partly to a general decline in church membership.

Related findings show that although seven teens in ten (70%) stress the importance of hard work, the percentage represents a significant drop since 1984 (82%).

Current valuations of personal integrity are higher, with about nine teens in ten placing great importance on responsibility (89%), honesty (89%) and self-respect (87%). Majorities of teens prize independence (65%), patience (61%) and obedience (60%).

Demographic Differences Pronounced

The importance of hard work among teens increases in large cities (78%), compared to youth in suburbs (69%) and rural areas (66%). Regionally, percentages are lowest in the East (65%) and highest in the South (72%). By religious affiliation, Protestant teens (73%) say they value the work ethic more so than Catholic youth (66%).

Honesty and responsibility are important to teens in all demographic strata and regions. Young women (90%), those 16 or older (90%) and teens living in the West (93%) especially value self-respect.

More younger teens (69%) than older (60%) value independence, while those living in large cities (72%) cite this quality more frequently than suburban or rural teens (at 64% and 63% respectively).

Gender differences factor considerably in attitudes toward patience, which young women cite by a margin of 64% to 59% of young men.

For a 52% majority of Protestant teens, religious faith is central. Thirty-seven percent of Catholic adolescents share this view. As would be expected, teens who attend church regularly (59%) are far more inclined than those who do not (25%) to emphasize the importance of faith. Among regions, percentages are proportionately higher in the Bible Belt states of the South (59%) and Midwest (42%) than in the West (38%) and East (32%).

THE SEXUAL REVOLUTION ENDING

Question:
There's a lot of discussion about the way morals and sexual attitudes are changing in this country. What is your opinion about this: Do you think it is wrong for a man and a woman to have sex relations before marriage, or not?

(Percent saying "wrong")

	1987 %	1985 %	1969 %
NATIONAL	46	39	68
Men	39	32	62
Women	53	44	74
18-29 years	27	18	49
30-49 years	41	35	67
50 and older	65	56	80
Protestants	52	46	70
Catholics	39	33	72

National Trends

	Wrong %	Not wrong %	No opinion %
1987	46	48	6
1985	39	52	9
1973	48	43	9
1969	68	21	11

Latest findings are based on personal interviews with 1,607 adults nationwide during July 1987.

Source: Gallup Poll

A recent Gallup survey indicates the sexual revolution of the last quarter-century may be coming to a halt, with a reversal in the dramatic trend since 1969 toward acceptance of premarital sex.

Between 1969 and 1985 the percentage of Americans who viewed premarital sex as wrong dropped a remarkable 29 percentage points, from 68% in the earlier survey to 39% in 1985. In the current survey, however, opposition has grown, with 46% now saying sex before marriage is wrong and about the same percentage, 48%, believing it is not .

The trend reversal may reflect growing concern over the risk of disease (such as herpes, AIDS, etc.), cited by one-fifth of those in the survey who object to premarital sex, largely on the basis of moral or religious reasons (named by 83%). Following these are risk of disease (20%), risk of pregnancy (13%), and the belief that women should be virgins before marriage (9%).

Women and older persons are more inclined than men and younger persons to say sex before marriage is wrong. Little difference in views is found by racial background.

Catholics today take a considerably more liberal view than Protestants, although in 1969 when the first survey was taken, Catholics and Protestants held similar views.

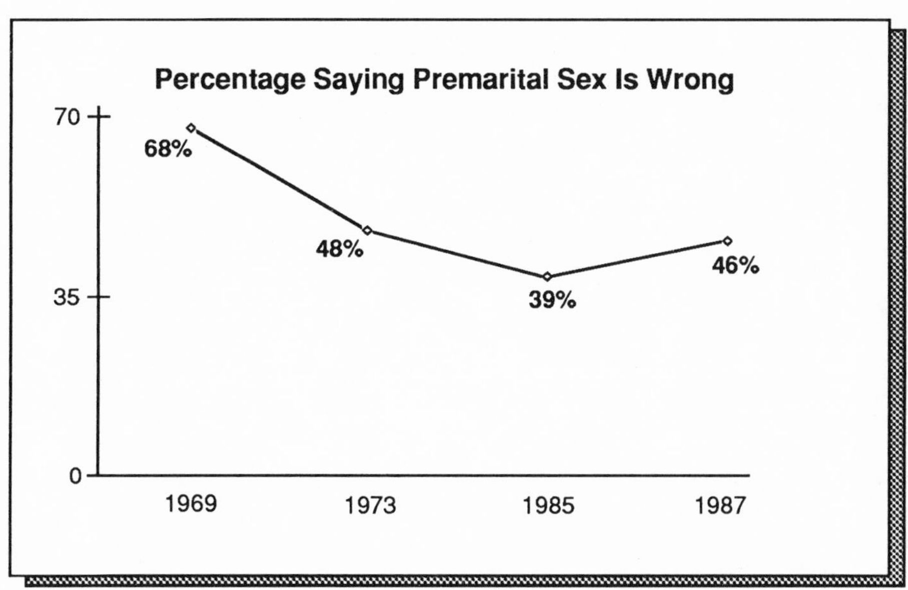

ATTITUDES ON ABORTION LITTLE CHANGED SINCE SUPREME COURT'S 1973 RULING

Question:
Do you think abortions should be legal under any circumstances, legal only under certain circumstances, or illegal under all circumstances?

	--- Legal ---		--- Illegal ---
	Any circumstances %	Certain circumstances %	All circumstances %
1988	24	57	17
1983	23	58	16
1981	23	52	21
1980	25	53	18
1979	22	54	19
1977	22	55	19
1975	21	54	22

Note: "No opinion" omitted.

Question:
Please tell me whether you think abortions should or should not be legal under each of the following circumstances: *If the woman's life is endangered? If the woman may suffer severe physical health damage? If there is a chance the baby will be born deformed? If the pregnancy is the result of rape or incest? If the family cannot affort to have the baby?*

	Approve %	Disapprove %	No Opinion %
Woman's life endangered	94	2	4
Rape or incest	85	11	4
Woman's health impaired	84	11	5
Baby born deformed	60	29	11
Can't afford child	19	75	6

Findings are based on telephone interviews with 1,001 adults nationwide during September 1988.

Source: Gallup Poll

Few issues in recent years have so sharply divided the American people as a woman's right to have an abortion. Yet public opinion on this issue has remained virtually unchanged since the Supreme Court's landmark 1973 decision upholding that right.

A 57% majority now favors legal abortions only under certain circumstances, while 24% back unlimited access, and 17% an outright ban. The latest findings are similar to those of earlier surveys. In 1975, for instance, 54% approved of abortions under certain conditions, 21% thought they should be legal under any circumstances, and 22% would make them illegal in all circumstances.

Large majorities of those who approve of abortions only under certain circumstances think they should be legal if the woman's life is endangered (94%), if the pregnancy results from rape or incest (85%), if the woman's physical health may be severely impaired (84%), and if there is a chance the baby will be deformed (60%). They reject abortions solely on economic grounds – if the family cannot afford to have the child – 75% to 19%.

Supreme Court Ruling

In 1973 the Supreme Court ruled that states cannot place restrictions on a woman's right to an abortion during the first three months of pregnancy. In the second trimester the states have no authority to prevent abortion but can regulate certain of the medical aspects involved. Only during the final trimester, when medical experts generally agree that the fetus is capable of living outside the womb, can states impose restrictions on a woman's right to an abortion.

Republicans, Democrats and Independents share almost identical opinions on the legality of abortions. Little difference is found on the basis of sex or age. Protestants and Catholics are in close agreement, although the Roman Catholic Church does not sanction abortions for any reason. Non-whites, Evangelicals, the less educated and less affluent hold more conservative opinions; whites, Non-evangelicals, college graduates, those with family incomes over $40,000 or more, Easterners and Westerners espouse more liberal views.

Opposition to the Reagan Administration's decision to block federal financing of family planning clinics that provide abortion counseling outweighed support, 66% to 26%, with majorities of Republicans (54%), Democrats (76%) and Independents (65%) disapproving of this decision.

STRATEGIES RANGE FOR WAR ON DRUGS

Question:
In your opinion, which of the following would do the most to halt the drug epidemic in the U.S.: Helping drug users to obtain treatment to overcome their dependency, making it harder for illegal drugs to get into the country, or educating young people and other nonusers about the dangers of drug abuse?

	Educating young people %	Harder to get drugs into country %	All equally (Vol.) %	Treatment for drug users %	None (Vol.) %	No opinion %
NATIONAL	47	35	13	6	1	2
Men	49	36	9	5	2	3
Women	45	35	16	7	1	2
18-29 years	52	29	9	11	1	1
30-49 years	49	32	16	6	1	1
50 and older	43	42	13	3	1	4
Whites	47	35	14	6	1	2
Blacks	44	36	5	11	1	5
College grads.	50	32	15	6	1	1
College inc.	43	31	20	6	1	2
H.S. grads.	49	40	11	5	1	2
Not H.S. grads.	46	36	4	9	6	2

Note: Totals exceed 100% due to multiple responses.

Findings are based on telephone interviews with 1,003 adults nationwide during March 1988.

Source: Gallup Poll

Beset by a rising flood of illegal drugs, Americans view anti-drug education of young people and efforts to halt foreign supplies as especially effective means of combating the epidemic.

Asked to choose among strategies for attacking the crisis, 47% favor educating young people, 35% emphasize interdiction of drugs, 6% stress treatment of drug users, and 13% support all of these tactics equally.

All demographic groups in the survey choose education as the primary tool, and place right behind it the need to keep drugs out of the country. Those under the age of 49 are slightly more likely than Americans over 50 to prefer education as the chief strategy; people over age 50 give greater weight to interdiction. Highest support for the drug treatment choice comes from blacks and people under 30.

Recent outbreaks of violence among gangs competing for the lucrative drug trade and various reports documenting the continuing influx of narcotics into this country have renewed attention on the immensity of the drug problem.

A central aspect of the current debate about fighting the crisis is whether it stems more from major drug suppliers or growing demand among American users. The survey indicates public attention is focused on both aspects of the problem and shows considerable support for a multi-faceted approach.

MOST CATHOLICS APPROVE A NEW SEXUAL ETHIC

Question:
Some people say that the official position of the Catholic Church on sexual morals should not be changed. Others say that this position should be changed to reflect trends in the modern world. Which point of view more closely reflects your own opinion?

	All Catholics %	Practicing* %	Non-practicing %
Should change	57	46	68
Should not	36	45	26
No opinion	7	9	6
	100 %	100 %	100 %

Question:
A Roman Catholic priest and professor of theology has been forbidden by the Vatican to teach theology on the basis that his teachings on sexual morals varied from the Vatican's official position. Have you heard or read about this?

About half of all Catholics (54%) were aware of the situation—including 69% of practicing and 39% of non-practicing Catholics.

All Catholics were then asked:

Question:
Do you agree or disagree with the Vatican's decision?

	All Catholics %	Practicing* %	Non-practicing %
Agree	32	47	16
Disagree	45	30	61
No opinion	23	23	23
	100 %	100 %	100 %

*Church members who attended Mass during the seven days prior to being interviewed and who describe religion as very important in their lives.

Findings are based on telephone interviews with 264 Roman Catholics out of a total sample of 978 adults nationwide during September 1986.

Source: Gallup Poll

In a climate of widely-publicized conflicts between liberal U.S. Catholic theologians and the Vatican, a majority of American Catholic laity would like their Church to adopt a more flexible polity on sexual morality.

In the latest Gallup Poll 57% of Roman Catholics said their Church should change its official position, while 36% believed the Church should adhere to its present polities on sexual ethics.

The impetus for change came mainly from Catholics less active in religious activities than from "practicing" Catholics, defined as Church members who attend Mass weekly and who describe religion as very important in their lives.

Among "practicing" Catholics, who comprise about half the total Catholic sample, public opinion was evenly divided between those who believe the Church should (46%) and should not (45%) change its position on sexual morality. For "non-practicing" Catholics, the heavy weight of opinion favored the Church's changing its stance to reflect trends in the modern world, 68% to 26%.

Curran's License Revoked

The survey was conducted shortly after the Vatican revoked the license of The Rev. Charles Curran, a Roman Catholic priest and university professor of theology, because his teachings on homosexuality, abortion, contraception, and other moral issues were at variance with Catholic dogma.

Catholics who disagreed with the Vatican's decision to censure Curran (45%) slightly outnumbered those who agreed (32%), with a large 23% undecided. Attitudes toward the Curran case, as on the broader issue of the Church's position on sexual morality, revealed the difference of opinion between practicing and non-practicing Catholics.

Among practicing Catholics, 47% agreed with the Vatican's decision, while 30% disagreed and 23% were undecided. Among the non-practicing group, only 16% agreed while 61% disagreed and, again, 23% were undecided.

V. Religion and Society

Americans uphold the tradition separating church and state, whose first proponent Baptist Roger Williams set a precedent for Thomas Jefferson and the Religion Clauses of the First Amendment. Today a total of 77% nationwide agree that church and state should be separate.

Since colonial times, however, civil religion has complicated the separation of religious issues from the nation's political matrix. In 1988 52% of the U.S. public felt that religious organizations should not lobby Congress to pass legislation, up from 45% in 1978. But in 1987 68% favored a constitutional amendment allowing prayer in public schools. Seventy-nine percent expressed support of public school instruction on world religions, permissible under constitutional law.

In recent years the vigorous interaction of religion and political life has done little to improve perceptions of religious impact on American society. Only 36% in 1988 thought religion was gaining influence in America, and half the population (49%) said it was decreasing. The figures are reversed from 1986, when 48% said "increasing" and 39% said "losing."

Even so, the influence of religion in American homes has been prevalent and largely positive. Seventy-two percent in 1986 agreed religion in the home had strengthened their families "a great deal" (35%) or "somewhat" (37%), while 94% in 1988 expressed satisfaction with family life.

Personal optimism ran almost as high that year, with 87% saying they were satisfied with their personal lives, roughly the same proportion recorded among all major religious and demographic groups except non-whites (79%). Satisfaction with the state of the nation rebounded to 56% in 1988 from 41% earlier in the year, ending the long aftermath of discontent that followed disclosures of the Iran-contra scandal and corruption on Capitol Hill. But non-whites were far less likely than whites to be satisfied with the nation, by a margin of 37% to 60%.

An estimated 31% of blacks in America live below the poverty level, nearly three times the number of whites (11%). In 1988 a 65% majority acknowledged that blacks still suffer discrimination, with considerable differences among black Protestants (73%), white Protestants (60%), and Catholics (66%) — despite overwhelming public support by 91% for equal opportunity.

Social justice has figured prominently in mainline religious agendas since the 1960s, but major religious groups today indicate about the same degree of concern as the general population for the hungry and homeless. Most Americans in 1988 (74%) agreed that government should care for those unable to care for themselves, statistically matching figures for Protestants (74%) and Catholics (73%). By 63% to 66%, though, slightly fewer Protestants than respondents nationwide felt that the government should guarantee every citizen shelter and enough to eat: an opinion shared among 71% of Catholics.

If generally satisfied with the state of the nation, Americans are growing less optimistic about organized religion. Fifty-nine percent expressed "a great deal" or "quite a lot" of confidence in the church during 1988, down from 66% in 1985. A huge majority of 92% in 1987 supported religious funding disclosures, up from 86% in 1980.

Growing skepticism toward the church may partly reflect the climate of opinion surrounding America's television ministers. Ethical breaches in the electronic church have generated a sharp uptrend in those who believe TV evangelists are dishonest, from 26% in 1980 to 53% in 1987. Ironically, their ratings improved between 1983 and 1987.

In terms of numbers the evangelical movement appears to have been unaffected by public scandals among TV evangelists. Thirty-three percent nationwide call themselves born-again or evangelical Christians, continuing the tradition inspired by eighteenth-century revivalists of the Great Awakenings.

RELIGIOUS INFLUENCE EBBING

Question:
At the present time, do you think religion as a whole is increasing its influence on American life or losing its influence?

	Increasing %	Losing %	Staying the Same %	No Opinion %
NATIONAL	36	49	6	9
Men	37	45	8	10
Women	34	52	5	9
18-29 years	40	51	4	5
30-49 years	38	49	6	7
50 and older	30	47	8	15
East	38	48	6	8
Midwest	39	45	7	9
South	31	53	4	12
West	36	48	9	7
Whites	35	48	7	10
Non-whites	36	54	6	4
Blacks	36	54	5	5
College grad.	38	48	9	5
College inc.	38	50	4	8
H.S. grad.	34	53	6	7
Not H.S. grad.	33	42	5	20
Protestants	34	49	6	11
Evangelicals	38	48	5	9
Non-evangelicals	35	49	7	9
Catholics	39	50	5	6

Findings are based on personal interviews with 1,003 adults nationwide during March 1988.

Source: Gallup Poll

The 1988 Gallup measure on religious impact shows a serious decline since 1986, from 48% to 36% who now say that religion is gaining influence on American life. Half of U.S. adults, 49%, think the influence of religion is decreasing, compared to 39% in 1986. The figures have reversed since 1986, when the number who cited a growing religious impact reached the highest level recorded in nearly three decades of this survey.

Of those who think the influence of religion is increasing, demographic shifts reveal significant downtrends between 1986 and 1988 among groups with strongest historic religious ties: women (47% to 34%), blacks (48% to 36%), Southerners (51% to 31%), and Protestants, who include the evangelical population (51% to 34%).

The religious impact measure is one of the most sensitive, and can change somewhat more rapidly than related indicators of the religious climate in America. Nevertheless, 1988 findings represent the sharpest downturn in religious influence since the 1960s, and suggest the current disaffection with organized religion is undermining its viability in the public square.

The Influence of Religion

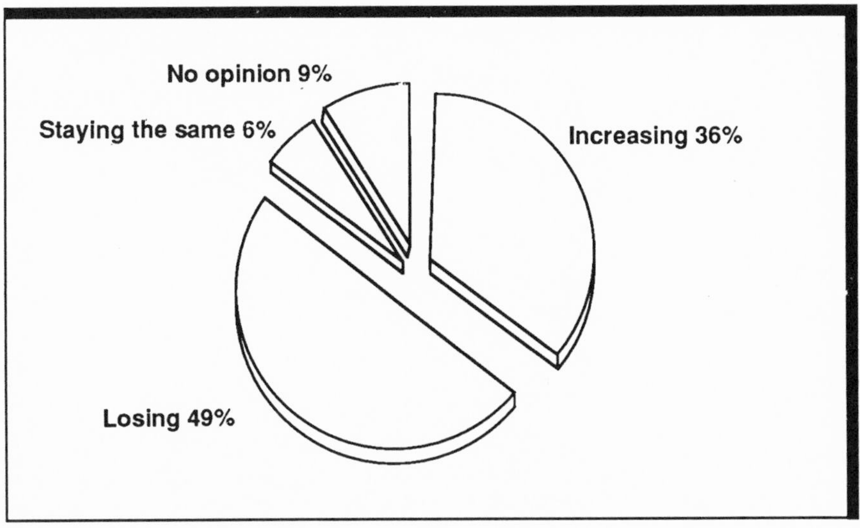

ORGANIZED RELIGION AMONG THE NATION'S MOST TRUSTED INSTITUTIONS

Question:
I am going to read you a list of institutions in American society. Please tell me how much confidence you, yourself, have in each one — a great deal, quite a lot, some, or very little?

(Percent saying "great deal" or "quite a lot")

	1988 %	1987 %	1985 %	1983 %	1979 %
Church or organized religion	59	61	66	62	65
Military	58	61	61	53	54
U.S. Supreme Court	56	52	56	42	45
Banks	49	51	51	51	60
Public Schools	49	50	48	39	53
Newspapers	36	31	35	38	51
Congress	35	*	39	28	34
Television	27	28	29	25	38
Organized labor	26	26	28	26	36
Big Business	25	*	31	28	32

*Not asked.

Latest findings are based on personal interviews with 1,030 adults nationwide during September 1988.

Source: Gallup Poll

Although public confidence in organized religion is slipping, the church shares a place with the military and the U.S. Supreme Court among selected institutions in which Americans have the greatest confidence.

Statistically equivalent numbers currently express "a great deal" or "quite a lot" of confidence in organized religion (59%), the military (58%) and the High Court (56%). While the Court has been among the top-rated institutions since the Gallup Poll began to monitor the public's confidence, the latest results mark the first time the Court has ranked squarely in the most respected group.

From 1973 until 1985 organized religion stood alone as the nation's most trusted institution, losing that distinction to the military the following year. Although religion has since registered an upturn in public confidence, it has failed to regain the primacy it formerly enjoyed. The military has declined slightly from its high point of 63% in 1986 but remains above its low of 50% in 1981. Confidence in the Supreme Court has increased by 14 percentage points since 1983, from 42% to 56% in 1985 and 1988.

Consistent with the results of earlier surveys, women, blacks, older Americans, Southerners, and the less well-educated currently express greater confidence in the church than do people from different socio-economic backgrounds.

Confidence in the Church Trends Downward

The following Gallup findings show the extent to which public confidence in the church or organized religion has trended downward over the last 15 years.

	Average %
Early 1970s (1973, 1975)	67
Late 1970s (1977, 1979)	64
Early 1980s (1981, 1983, 1984, 1985)	64
Late 1980s (1986, 1987, 1988)	59

AMERICANS SUPPORT SEPARATION OF CHURCH AND STATE

Question:

I am going to read you [a] statement about religion and politics, and . . . I'd like you to tell me whether you completely agree with it, mostly agree with it, mostly disagree with it, or completely disagree with it.

In our system of government, church and state should be separated.

	Completely agree %	Mostly agree %	Mostly disagree %	Completely disagree %	Don't know %
NATIONAL	48	29	12	5	6

Findings are based on personal interviews with 2,109 adults nationwide during January 1988.
Source: Gallup Poll

Question:

Do you agree or disagree with this statement:

Religious organizations should persuade senators and representatives to enact legislation on ethical and moral issues they would like to see become law.

	Agree %	Disagree %	No Opinion %
NATIONAL	35	52	13
Catholics	33	53	14
Protestants	41	48	11
Southern Baptists	48	35	17
Baptists	44	42	14
Methodists	36	52	12
Lutherans	43	48	9
Presbyterians	40	52	8
Evangelicals	53	36	11
Non-evangelicals	27	61	12

*Less than one percent.

Findings are based on personal interviews with 1,030 adults nationwide during October 1988.
Source: Gallup Poll

According to a 1988 pre-election poll, Americans overwhelmingly support the principle of separation of church and state, by a combined total of 79%. Public opinion is mixed, however, on whether one branch of society can attempt to persuade another while remaining separate, as suggested by response to the question of whether religious organizations should influence actions of Congress.

In 1988 35% of U.S. citizens felt that religious organizations should exercise a role in advocating national legislation on ethical and moral issues. The 1988 finding represents a drop from 41% recorded in 1978. Conversely, since 1978 an uptrend has occurred (45% to 52%) among those who disagree that religious organizations should affect national legislation.

Patterns of response among demographic groups generally reflect current national figures, but many religious groups differ considerably from the general population. Protestants — especially Baptists, Southern Baptists, Lutherans and Evangelicals — are more likely than the U.S. public to support religious influence on the law. Opinion against such measures is stronger among Non-evangelicals than Americans nationwide.

MAJORITY FAVOR AMENDMENT FOR SCHOOL PRAYER

Question:
Do you favor or oppose an amendment to the U.S. Constitution that would allow prayer in the public schools?

	NATIONAL %	No children in schools %	Public school parents %
Favor	68	68	69
Oppose	26	26	26
Don't know	6	6	6

Findings are based on personal interviews with 1,571 nationwide during April 1987.

Source: 19th Annual Gallup Poll/Phi Delta Kappa Survey

Electorate

Question:
Are you more or less likely to vote for a candidate who opposes a constitutional amendment permitting prayer in public schools?

	More Likely %	Less Likely %
NATIONAL	30	70

Findings are based on personal interviews with 2,109 adults nationwide during June 1988.

Source: Gallup Poll for *Times Mirror*

Teens

Question:
Do you favor or oppose prayer in the schools?

	1987	1985	1981
	%	%	%
Favor	55	60	45
Oppose	31	31	43
No opinion	14	9	12

Findings are based on telephone interviews with 509 teenagers 13 to18 nationwide during 1987.

Source: Gallup Youth Survey

The issue of school prayer has been hotly debated since the 1962 Supreme Court ruling that organized prayer in public schools is not permissible under the First Amendment. During his administration, Ronald Reagan joined many in calling for a constitutional amendment to allow school prayer.

The American public strongly supports school prayer. Seventy-eight percent are aware of the fact that an amendment to the U.S. Constitution has been proposed allowing school prayer. Within that group 68% favor the amendment, and 26% oppose it. Almost three-fourths of the total sample (71%) feel that only a small percentage of the population would be offended by school prayer.

Voters Support Prayer in Schools

Seventy percent of all Americans expressing an opinion say they would be less likely to vote for a candidate who opposes a constitutional amendment permitting prayer in public schools. Voters take this position regardless of their political views: Democrats are as likely as GOP voters to reject a candidate who opposes a school prayer amendment.

Even the electorate's one non-religious voter group — tolerant, non-militant "Seculars," as defined in a poll for *Times Mirror* — split evenly on the issue, with 51% saying "less likely" and 49% saying "more likely."

Most Teens Approve of School Prayer

Fifty-five percent of the nation's teens favor a time for prayer in schools, with 31% opposed and 14% undecided. Support for school prayer among teens has weakened since 1985 when 60% favored the idea. In a 1981 survey substantially fewer teens who favored prayer (45%) were divided evenly against those who opposed (43%). Related Gallup surveys in 1985 found greatest support among adults, 69% of whom favored prayer in schools.

AMERICANS WANT RELIGION IN SCHOOLS

Question:
Here are some questions about the Bible, including both Old and New Testaments. Please tell me whether you would or would not object to the public schools . . .

	Would not object %	Would object %	No opinion %
Teaching about the major religions of the world	79	16	5
Using the Bible in literature, history and social studies classes	75	20	5
Making facilities available after school hours for use by student religious groups or organizations	74	21	5
Offering elective courses in Bible studies	75	20	5

Findings are based on personal interviews with 1,559 adults nationwide during October 1986.

Source: Gallup Survey as a public service with the Laymen's National Bible Association

By overwhelming margins, Americans would like to see public schools offer a variety of religious studies such as elective Bible courses and study of the Bible in literature, history, social studies and comparative religion.

A large majority also favors making school facilities available for use by student religious groups during non-school hours.

Unlike school prayer, which the Supreme Court has prohibited on constitutional grounds, the activities cited in this poll are permissible under the First Amendment.

Heavy Support in all Regions

The survey found no significant difference in public opinion toward school participation in each activity. Seventy-nine percent expressed no objection to teaching major world religions, and 75% did not object to Bible study courses and using scriptures in conjunction with secular studies. Seventy-four percent would not object to making school facilities available for student religious organizations. Similarly, the percent objecting to each of these actions ranges only between 16% and 21% nationwide.

Among all national regions and in every major population group, heavy public support obtains for each of the activities named. However, a 1987 Gallup International Poll shows Americans are considerably less likely than citizens of most countries surveyed to support religion in public schools.

With the exception of comparative religion courses, to which no more than one in six in any group objects, college graduates are slightly more likely than those with less formal education to object to schools undertaking the activities surveyed. Nevertheless, support strongly outweighs opposition among college graduates as well as non-graduates.

A THIRD OF U.S. ADULTS BORN-AGAIN EVANGELICALS

Question:
Would you describe yourself as a "born-again" or evangelical Christian, or not?

	Yes %	No %	No Opinion %
NATIONAL	33	63	4
Men	29	67	4
Women	37	59	4
18-29 years	30	66	4
30-49 years	31	66	3
50 and older	39	57	4
East	21	75	4
Midwest	32	64	4
South	49	47	4
West	26	70	4
Whites	31	65	4
Non-whites	49	47	4
Blacks	57	40	3
Hispanics	24	68	8
College grad.	22	76	2
College inc.	31	66	3
H.S. grad.	35	61	4
Not H.S. grad.	45	49	6
$40,000 and over	25	73	2
$25,000 - $39,999	33	64	3
$15,000 - $24,999	35	60	5
Under $15,000	40	55	5
Protestants	49	48	3
Catholics	12	83	5

Findings are based on telephone and personal interviews with 5,045 adults nationwide during 1988.

Source: Gallup Poll

More than one-third of U.S. adults are taking part in the evangelical movement, which cuts across denominations and shares a prominent place in the nation's religious mainstream. By definition an evangelical or born-again Christian believes the Bible is the word of God and reads it regularly, has experienced personal conversion, and seeks to lead non-Christians to conversion.

A Gallup Survey conducted in 1988 found that 33% nationwide call themselves born-again or evangelical Christians, statistically the same proportion recorded in 1986 (33%) and a decade earlier in 1976 (34%). Most recent findings revealed no significant shift in the composition of Evangelicals, disproportionately Protestant, southern, black and poor, but visibly represented among all demographic groups.

By a margin of 37% to 29% more women than men call themselves Evangelicals, whose ranks also include more adults 50 and older (39%) than those 30 to 49 (31%) and 18 to 29 (30%). While the South claims half the born-again population (49%), large minorities reside in the Midwest (32%), the West (26%) and the East (21%).

Over half of Evangelicals are black (57%), compared to 49% of non-whites, 31% of whites and 24% of Hispanics. Adults without a high school diploma comprise 45% of Evangelicals, represented among 35% of high school graduates, 31% of adults with some college education and 22% of college graduates. One in four born-again Christians (40%) earn less than $15,000 a year, with 25% at $40,000 or more.

Half of American Protestants (49%) are self-described Evangelicals, four times the proportion of Catholics (12%).

MORAL MAJORITY FACES OPPOSITION, APATHY

Question:
Please tell me how you feel about each of the following:

. . . the activities of the Moral Majority.

	Favor %	Oppose %	No Opinion %
NATIONAL	28	39	33
Men	29	41	30
Women	27	38	35
Conservative religious ideology	45	27	28
Moderate	30	40	30
Liberal	17	58	25
Protestants	30	39	31
Catholics	26	37	37
Evangelicals	36	26	38
Non-evangelicals	26	43	31

Findings are based on personal interviews with 1,522 adults nationwide during June 1984.

Source: Gallup Survey for the Robert H. Schuller Ministries

During the late seventies Rev. Jerry Falwell conducted a national mailing campaign that launched the Moral Majority — now called the Liberty Foundation — a fundamentalist political movement organized to influence Congress on issues such as abortion, homosexuality, school prayer and military spending. Falwell's involvement with PTL alienated many of his followers, while his controversial support of the white ruling party in South Africa has intensified his opposition.

Public opinion of the Moral Majority is more negative than positive, but sharp differences polarize respondents on the basis of whether they consider themselves conservative, moderate or liberal in their religious beliefs.

When asked about their feelings toward the Moral Majority, 39% of U.S. citizens opposed the movement and 28% signaled support; 33% offered no opinion. Men were somewhat more inclined than women to oppose by a margin of 41% to 38%, although more women than men offered no opinion by 35% to 30%.

Religious conservatives (45%) were most likely to favor Falwell's efforts, compared to moderates (30%) and liberals (17%). Conversely, 58% of liberals opposed, as did 40% of moderates and 27% of conservatives.

The Moral Majority has never commanded the majority of born-again Christians or Evangelicals, whose supporting numbers (36%) divided evenly among those without an opinion (38%); one-fourth (26%) expressed disfavor. Non-evangelicals reported far greater opposition than support by 43% to 26%.

In addition more Protestants responded negatively (39%) than positively (30%), while opposing Catholics (37%) similarly outweighed those favoring the movement (26%).

ELECTRONIC CHURCH SCANDALS ROCK TV MINISTRIES

Question:
Here is a list of terms, shown as pairs of opposites, that have been used to describe television evangelists or ministers. From each pair of opposites, would you select the term you feel best describes television evangelists or ministers, in general?

	1987 %	1980 %
Care about people	48	59
Don't care about people	38	21
No opinion	14	20
Honest	34	53
Dishonest	53	26
No opinion	13	21
Sincere	34	56
Insincere	51	25
No opinion	15	19
Have a special relationship with God	30	47
Do not have a special relationship with God	56	33
No opinion	14	20
Trustworthy with money	23	41
Not trustworthy with money	63	36
No opinion	14	23

Latest findings are based on personal interviews with 1,571 adults nationwide during April 1987

Source: Gallup Poll

The corruption that has rocked TV ministries in recent months, and the subsequent power struggle within their ranks, have cast a long shadow over many of the nation's most popular TV evangelists and the evangelical movement in general. The cause of organized religion as a whole may have been harmed by the problems that have beset the electronic church.

Revelations of wrongdoing have damaged popular stereotypes of TV evangelists. Far fewer now than in 1980 perceive them to be trustworthy, honest, sincere and caring. In addition more now question their "special relationship with God" than seven years ago.

Key findings show:

- In the current survey perceptions of TV evangelists as "untrustworthy" outweigh "trustworthy" by 63% to 23%. In 1980 a 41% plurality held positive views, while 36% were negative.

- Today TV ministers are said to be "honest" by 34%, "dishonest" by 53%. In 1980 honest outnumbered dishonest by 53% to 26%.

- Currently 34% feel TV evangelists are "sincere," 51% that they are "insincere." In 1980 sincere ratings prevailed by 56% to 25%.

- Forty-eight percent now believe TV evangelists "care about people," while 38% feel they do not. In 1980 "caring" outweighed "not caring" by almost a 3-to-1 ratio, 59% to 21%.

- At present a 56% majority thinks TV evangelists do not have a "special relationship with God," while 30% believe they do. In 1980 a strong 47% plurality felt they were endowed with this relationship; 33% disagreed.

As expected, self-described evangelical Christians (27% of the total sample) hold generally more favorable opinions than Non-evangelicals on each of the five stereotypes. However, 47% of Evangelicals currently describe TV evangelists as untrustworthy, 35% as dishonest, 33% as insincere, 26% as uncaring, and 38% say they do not have a special relationship with God.

RELIGIOUS TV AUDIENCE GROWS

Question:
Do you ever watch religious programs on television?
Those who responded affirmatively, 49% of the total, were asked:
In the past 30 days, have you watched any religious programs on television?
Viewers within the last 30 days, 39% of the total, were then asked:
In the past 7 days, have you watched any religious programs on television?

	1987 %	1983 %
Total viewers	49	42
Within past 7 days	25	18
Within past 8-30 days	14	14
31 days or more	10	10
Non-viewers	51	58
	100 %	100 %

	Total viewers %	Last 7 days %	8-30 days %	31 days or more %	Non-viewers %
NATIONAL	49	25	14	10	51
Evangelicals	79	46	19	14	21
Non-evangelicals	36	15	12	9	64
Men	44	21	13	10	56
Women	53	29	15	9	47
Whites	46	23	13	10	54
Blacks	68	39	18	11	32
18-29 years	39	18	11	10	61
30-49 years	47	22	15	10	53
50 and over	58	33	15	10	42

Latest findings are based on personal interviews with 1,571 adults nationwide during April 1987.

Source: Gallup Poll

About half of American adults (49%) at least occasionally watch religious TV programs, and one-fourth (25%) view weekly: a huge audience that ranges among all generations and cuts across denominations.

Not surprisingly, self-described Evangelicals are the most loyal viewers, with eight in ten (79%) saying they sometimes watch religious television and almost half (46%) watching weekly. At least one-third of Non-evangelicals (36%) also watch these programs, although they tend to be less frequent viewers.

Among Evangelicals, disproportionately heavy viewing occurs among women, blacks, people 50 and older, the less affluent and less well educated, those from blue-collar occupational backgrounds, and Southerners.

Despite ethical breaches among some prominent TV evangelists, the audience for religious programming appears to have grown slightly since 1983 when the last study was conducted, with total viewership up from 42% four years ago. All growth traces to an increase from 18% to 25% in weekly viewers.

NINETY-TWO PERCENT FAVOR RELIGIOUS FUNDING DISCLOSURES

Question:
Do you agree or disagree with each of the following statements?

Religious organizations should make full disclosure of the funds they receive and how they are spent.

	1987 %	1980 %
Agree	92	86
Disagree	5	7
Not sure	3	7

The federal government should regulate the fundraising activities of religious organizations.

	1987 %	1980 %
Agree	43	35
Disagree	49	54
Not sure	8	11

Giving money to religious causes or organizations is more important than giving money to other causes.

	1987 %	1980 %
Agree	14	28
Disagree	81	61
Not sure	5	11

Latest findings are based on personal interviews with 1,571 adults nationwide during April 1987.

Source: Gallup Poll

Recent financial scandals involving the $2 billion electronic church have strengthened public demands for government regulation of religious fundraising and disclosure of the disposition of these funds.

Diminished public confidence in television ministries has generated a growing demand for regulation. In 1980 disagreement outweighed agreement that "the federal government should regulate the fundraising activities of religious organizations," by a 3 to 2 ratio. In the current survey opposition to regulation prevails, but by a narrower margin of 49% to 43%.

In addition there is virtually unanimous agreement (92%) that "religious organizations should make full disclosure of the funds they receive and how they are spent."

Substantially fewer now (14%) than in 1980 (28%) agree that "giving money to religious causes or organizations is more important than giving money to other causes." Eighty-one percent nationwide disagree, an opinion held among majorities of all population groups, including Evangelicals, viewers of religious TV programs, and donors to TV evangelists.

RELIGION STRENGTHENS THE AMERICAN FAMILY

Question:
To what extent, if at all, has religion in your home strengthened family relationships—a great deal, somewhat, hardly at all, or not at all?

	1986 %	1980 %
A great deal	35	39
Somewhat	37	35
Hardly at all	16	12
Not at all	10	11
No opinion	2	3
	100 %	100 %

Question:
How satisfied would you say you are with your own family life at this time — would you say you are very satisfied, mostly satisfied, mostly dissatisfied, or very dissatisfied with your family life at this time?

	1986 %	1980 %
Very satisfied	45	47
Mostly satisfied	48	44
Mostly dissatisfied	3	6
Very dissatisfied	2	2
No opinion	2	1
	100 %	100 %

Latest findings are based on telephone interviews with 504 adults nationwide during October 1986.

Source: In 1986, Gallup Poll; in 1980, Gallup Survey for the White House Conference on Families

Despite the alarming divorce rate in the U.S. , almost as many Americans in 1986 as in 1980 said they are "very satisfied" with family life, by 45% to 47%.

About equal proportions in 1986 as in 1980 felt they were "very" and "mostly" satisfied, and few in either survey reported being mostly or very dissatisfied. However, younger persons and those with relatively little formal education were less likely than their counterparts to say they were very satisfied with family life.

Impact of Religion on Families

A large majority of Americans, 72%, believe that religion has strengthened family relationships either "a great deal" or "somewhat." Only about one in four (26%) say religion has played such a role "hardly at all" or "not at all."

Perceptions of the impact of religion on the family have changed little since 1980. By contrast, considerable change was found on a related question concerning perceptions of other families. A higher proportion in 1986 said the family life of most people they know has improved, by a margin of 53% to 37% in 1980.

PUBLIC AND PERSONAL SATISFACTION RUNNING HIGH

Question:
In general, are you satisfied or dissatisfied with the way things are going in the U. S. at this time?

(Percent Satisfied)

NATIONAL	56 %
Men	62
Women	52
Whites	60
Non-whites	37
Protestants	55
Evangelicals	50
Non-evangelicals	60
Catholics	64

Question:
Please tell me whether you are satisfied or dissatisfied with the following aspects of your life....

(Percent Satisfied)

	Family Life %	Health %	Free Time %	Housing %	Standard of living %	Job %	House-hold Income %
NATIONAL	94	88	87	87	85	76	69
Protestants	93	86	89	87	85	74	67
Evangelicals	93	85	87	86	85	74	65
Non-evangelicals	94	91	86	88	85	78	71
Catholics	96	92	85	87	86	81	74

Findings are based on telephone interviews with 1,001 adults nationwide during September/October 1988.

Source: Gallup Poll

Public satisfaction with the state of the nation rebounded in 1988 to 56%, the highest figure recorded since December 1986 following disclosure of the Iran-contra debacle, a factor in the downturn to 47%. The national figure had reached a seven-year peak of 66% in March 1986 when consumers were extremely bullish about their financial prospects. At that time almost four in ten (37%) said they were better off than they had been a year earlier, and expected to be still more prosperous a year hence.

Latest results show the public mood at its brightest in two years, although a substantial minority of four in ten (40%) are dissatisfied with the country's state of affairs. While fewer women than men say they are satisfied (52% to 62%), those least content with the nation are non-whites (37%), Americans 50 and older (47%), persons without a high school diploma (47%), and those earning less than $15,000 a year (43%).

Among religious groups Catholics are the most optimistic about the nation, with 64% satisfied, compared to 55% of Protestants, 50% of Evangelicals, and 60% of Non-evangelicals.

Satisfaction With Personal Life at a High Point

Personal satisfaction in America has been on an upward trend since the recession of the early 1980s. Gallup began asking Americans whether they are satisfied with their lives in 1979, and at no time since then has this measure topped the 87% recorded in the latest survey.

Moreover, the public is more content with basic aspects of their lives than in many years. Solid and growing majorities of citizens express satisfaction with each of seven key dimensions of their lives. Satisfaction with family life has grown from 88% to 94% in the last four years, while over the same period of time satisfaction with health has increased from 85% to 88%; leisure time, from 78% to 87%; housing, from 81% to 87%; standard of living, from 78% to 85%; jobs, from 70% to 76%; and household income, from 63% to 69%.

On most items general levels of satisfaction are high for both whites and blacks, but some sharp differences exist. Only 52% of blacks are satisfied with their household income, compared to 71% of whites. Marked differences appear also for standard of living and housing.

By and large, religious groups express similar degrees of satisfaction on these items. However, Catholics are slightly more inclined than their counterparts to say they are content with their families, health, jobs, and household income.

DISCRIMINATION AGAINST BLACKS CALLS FOR MORAL REDRESS

Question:
Now I am going to read you a series of statements that will help us understand how you feel about a number of things. For each statement, please tell me whether you completely agree with it, mostly agree with it, mostly disagree with it or completely disagree with it.

	Completely Agree %	Mostly Agree %	Mostly Disagree %	Completely Disagree %	No Opinion %
Our society should do what is necessary to make sure that everyone has an equal *opportunity* to succeed.	48	43	6	1	2
	91		7		
In the past few years there hasn't been much real improvement in the position of black people in this country.	12	25	41	18	4
	37		59		
Discrimination against blacks is rare today.	7	25	41	24	3
	32		65		

Findings are based on personal interviews with 3,021 adults nationwide during May 1988.

Source: Gallup Survey for *Times Mirror*

In 1988 the U.S. Senate approved a bill to enforce housing discrimination laws first enacted under the 1965 Civil Rights Act. The bill underscores actions taken during the 1960s to insure equal opportunity in America, now supported by an overwhelming majority of 91%.

According to the latest Gallup Poll conducted for *Times Mirror,* most citizens (65%) disagree that discrimination is rare against blacks, for whom the civil rights laws were originally written two decades ago. Conversely, 59% suggest the position of blacks has improved over the past few years, despite signs of a resurgence of racism in America.

Perceptions Vary on Blacks' Position

Majorities affirming equal opportunity in all demographic and religious groups vary no more than three percentage points from the national average of 91%. Responses range widely, however, on perceptions of blacks in America today.

While 59% disagree that "there hasn't been much real improvement in the position of blacks in this country," disparities among races are vast. Seventy percent of blacks agree with the statement, compared to 33% of whites and 63% of non-whites.

Although 36% of all Protestants say that blacks have not seen recent gains, white and black Protestants differ sharply by a margin of 30% to 70%. Evangelicals and Non-evangelicals agree by 26% to 32%, fewer than Catholics and Jews who agree by 36% to 43%.

Twenty-nine percent of Republicans report no real improvements among U.S. blacks, a perception held more strongly among Democrats (45%) and Independents (35%).

Discrimination Against Blacks Still Widespread

Majorities of all population groups disagree that "discrimination against blacks is rare today," although blacks (75%), non-whites (69%) and Hispanics (70%) dissent more frequently than whites (66%).

Similar patterns occur among religious groups: black Protestants (73%) are most likely to cite the prevalence of discrimination toward their numbers. The figure represents a sizable gap between all Protestants (62%), particularly white Protestants (60%) who disagree that racism is rare. Fewer Evangelicals (56%) than Non-evangelicals (63%) share this opinion, while Catholics (66%) and Jews (79%) express greater disagreement.

AMERICANS FAVOR PUBLIC SUPPORT FOR THE HUNGRY AND HOMELESS

Question:

Now I am going to read you a series of statements that will help us understand how you feel about a number of things. For each statement, please tell me whether you completely agree with it, mostly agree with it, mostly disagree with it or completely disagree with it.

	Completely Agree %	Mostly Agree %	Mostly Disagree %	Completely Disagree %	No Opinion %
It is the responsibility of the government to take care of people who can't take care of themselves.	26	48	17	6	3
	74		23		
The government should help more needy people even if it means going deeper into debt.	17	35	30	12	6
	52		42		
The government should guarantee every citizen enough to eat and a place to sleep.	28	38	22	9	3
	66		31		

Findings are based on personal interviews with 3,021 adults nationwide during May 1988.

Source: Gallup Survey for *Times Mirror*

The biblical injunction to care for the poor and hungry is well attested in the Hebrew Bible and New Testament. While many religious communities are responding to the plight of disenfranchised and homeless Americans, majorities across denominations are calling for a cooperative effort from the federal government: an effort favored among most voters as well.

Homelessness in America has reached staggering proportions, especially among low-income families affected by drastic cuts in federal housing assistance. According to a report in *The Yale Review* by Jonathan Kozol, the homeless population of an estimated two to three million now includes about a half million dependent children.

Seventy-four percent nationwide think the government is responsible for those unable to care for themselves; 52% say public assistance to the needy should prevail over a resulting rise of the national debt. In addition 66% believe the government "should guarantee every citizen enough to eat and a place to sleep."

Protestants support federal provisions for food and shelter by 63%, with 59% of white Protestants and 81% of black Protestants agreeing. Fifty-nine percent of Evangelicals favor such measures, as compared to 61% of Non-evangelicals and 71% of Catholics.

Among those who feel the national debt is secondary to increased aid to the needy, Protestants agree by 53% — 48% white and 76% black — while 49% of Evangelicals, 48% of Non-evangelicals and 54% of Catholics respond in kind.

All religious groups share the opinion that the government has a duty toward people without means to care for themselves. Seventy-four percent of Protestants agree; 72% of whites and 82% of blacks. Evangelicals (73%), Non-evangelicals (72%) and Catholics (73%) answer similarly.

VI. Religious Experience

A striking number of Americans, one-third in 1988, reported having a "powerful religious insight or awakening" at some time in their lives. In a related survey conducted that year, 81% agreed "completely" or "mostly" that they are "sometimes very conscious of the presence of God,"about as many who said in 1986 that they had received divine guidance in the course of their lives (83%).

These experiences increase with age, and are more pronounced among Evangelicals, who believe Christians must undergo spiritual rebirth and, since the Great Awakenings, have shared a piety that many today express politically. Contemporary evangelicalism has been gaining momentum in America since the early 1970s, and results indicate its influence extends well beyond such traditionally evangelical churches as the Southern Baptist Convention. Thirty-eight percent of the general population had undergone a "born-again" experience in 1982, compared to a full 100% of Evangelicals. A considerable minority of Catholics (21%) reported the born-again experience.

Experiences of God clearly occur widely outside evangelical communities. Seventy-nine percent of self-described Non-evangelicals agreed in 1988 that they are "sometimes very conscious of the presence of God," suggesting the extent to which Americans seek and experience the divine without reference to evangelical theology.

SPIRITUAL 'AWAKENING' TOUCHES ONE-THIRD OF AMERICANS

Question:
Have you ever had a religious experience—that is, a particularly powerful religious insight or awakening?

	Yes %	No %	No opinion %
NATIONAL	33	63	4
Men	30	67	3
Women	36	60	4
Whites	33	64	3
Blacks	40	55	5
Hispanics	27	70	3
18-24 years	24	72	4
25-29 years	32	64	4
30-49 years	37	61	2
50 and older	33	62	5
Protestants	41	55	4
Catholics	24	74	2
Churched	40	56	4
Unchurched	25	72	3

Findings are based on personal interviews with 2,556 adults nationwide during March 1988.

Source: Gallup Survey for the National Catholic Evangelization Association

Psychologist of religion William James thought that individual experience of the "unseen order" built the foundations of all world religions. According to Oxford biologist David Hay, James' comment may point more to physiology than speculation. Director of the Alister Hardy Research Center, Dr. Hay believes mystical awareness is so prevalent that it is "biologically natural" to the human organism.

A third of Americans (33%) say they have undergone a "powerful religious insight or awakening" at some point in their lives, an event most frequently cited between the ages of 30 and 40 (37%) and among blacks (40%). Total national findings have not changed significantly since 1978 when 35% reported a religious experience and 64% did not.

Thirty-six percent of women say they have had a religious awakening or insight, compared to 30% of men. Protestants claim this experience by 41% to 24% of Catholics, and churchgoers by 40% to 25% of unchurched Americans.

CONSCIOUSNESS OF GOD PREVALENT

Question:
How much do you agree or disagree with the following statement?

I am sometimes very conscious of the presence of God.

	Completely Agree %	Mostly Agree %	Mostly Disagree %	Completely Disagree %	No Opinion %
NATIONAL	46	35	11	5	3
Men	38	37	15	6	4
Women	53	33	9	3	2
Under 30 years	39	40	12	5	4
30-49 years	44	34	13	6	3
50 and older	53	31	10	3	3
Whites	44	36	12	5	3
Blacks	62	29	6	1	2
Hispanics	56	30	8	4	2
Protestants	52	34	10	2	2
White Protestants	51	35	10	2	2
Black Protestants	64	29	6	1	*
Evangelicals	75	21	3	*	1
Non-evangelicals	34	45	15	3	3
Catholics	42	41	11	3	3

*Less than one percent.

Findings are based on personal interviews with 2,556 adults nationwide during May 1988.

Source: Gallup Survey for *Times Mirror*

A total of eight in ten Americans (81%) agree that they are "sometimes very conscious of the presence of God," with far fewer, 16%, who say they are not.

Women "completely agree" to this statement far more frequently than men by 53% to 38%; only 12% of women and 21% of men disagree.

Persons over 50 are most likely to say they are conscious of God's presence (84%), compared to 78% of respondents between 30 and 49 and roughly the same number under 30 (79%).

In terms of race, blacks (91%) are considerably more likely than whites (80%) and Hispanics (86%) to agree. Only 7% of blacks, 17% of whites and 12% of Hispanics indicate little or no awareness of God's presence.

By religious affiliation, evangelical Protestants (96%) are most inclined to report awareness of a divine presence, compared to 79% of Non-evangelicals. Eighty-six percent of all Protestants say they are sometimes very conscious of God, though black Protestants agree more frequently than white Protestants by 93% to 86%. Eighty-three percent of Catholics respond similarly.

REMARKABLE 43% REPORT AWARENESS OF GOD

Question:
Have you ever been aware of, or influenced by, a presence or a power—whether you call it God or not—which is different from your everyday self?

(Percent feeling presence)

NATIONAL	43 %
Men	38
Women	47
18-29 years	36
30-49 years	47
50 and older	42
Protestants	48
Catholics	37
Southern Baptists	52
Methodists	48
Lutherans	43

Descriptions of Spiritual Presence
(Based on those feeling presence)

Presence of God	21 %
Guidance, help from God	11
Indescribable feeling	11
Calming, comforting	10
Contentment, peace, well-being	7
At time of illness	6
Answer to prayer	6
Like ESP, intuition	5
Guardian	4
Gave me strength	3
Conscience	3
A light	2
All others	6
Don't know	5
	100 %

Results are based on personal interviews with 1,525 adults nationwide during April 1985.

Source: Gallup Survey for the Religious Education Association of the United States and Canada

In 1985 the late Sir Alister Hardy, an Oxford marine biologist, received the Templeton Prize for Progress in Religion and for his collection and analysis of extraordinary religious experiences. His hypothesis that religious awareness is innate to the human species led him to believe that knowledge of spiritual experience would reduce conflict among world religions.

A nationwide Gallup Poll has determined that a remarkable 43% of Americans report unusual and inexplicable spiritual or religious experiences of profound and positive impact, ranging from out-of-body travel to visionary encounters.

In the same survey by the Gallup affiliate in Great Britain, 33% reported spiritual experiences, a figure nearly identical to the percentage recorded in an earlier study by the Religious Experience Research Unit at Manchester College, Oxford (now the Alister Hardy Research Center).

U.S. findings show that women are more likely than men to report such experiences, as well as persons over 30, the college educated, and those for whom religion is very important.

Descriptions of spiritual experiences include a sense of divine presence and guidance, peace, extrasensory perception, answered prayer and renewed strength.

BORN-AGAIN EXPERIENCE PERVADES

Question:
Would you say that you have been born-again or have had a born-again experience—that is, a turning point in your life when you committed yourself to Jesus Christ? Was this a sudden experience, a gradual experience, or both?

	National %	Catholic %	Protestant %	Evangelical %
Yes	38	21	52	100
Sudden	8	3	11	24
Gradual	20	14	27	48
Both	10	4	15	27
No opinion	*	*	*	*
No	53	71	7	*
No opinion	9	8	7	*
	100 %	100 %	100 %	100 %.

*Less than one half of one percent.

Findings are based on personal interviews with 2,669 adults nationwide during December 1982.

Source: Gallup Survey for the Robert H. Schuller Ministries

Nearly two out of five Americans (38%) cite a born-again experience or conversion and renewal of the spirit in Christ. For most of these, the experience came about gradually; especially among Evangelicals, who by definition are born-again and thus report the experience by 100%.

Although the charismatic movement originated in the Catholic Church, only 21% of Catholics say they have been born again, far less than Protestants at a staggering 52%.

More likely to experience renewal are women, the elderly, married adults and non-whites. Those who consider religion very important, who believe Jesus was God and make the greatest possible effort to follow his example are more likely to say they have been born-again.

MOST GIVE SERIOUS THOUGHT TO SELF WORTH, FAITH

Question:
How much have you *thought* about the following during the past two years: a lot, a fair amount, only a little, or not at all?

Your relation to God
Living a worthwhile life
Developing your faith
The basic meaning and value of your life

	A Lot %	Fair Amount %	A Little %	Not at All %	No Opinion %
Living a worthwhile life	67	20	9	3	1
Your relation to God	59	20	15	5	1
The basic meaning and value of your life	58	24	13	4	1
Developing your faith	47	21	20	11	1

Findings are based on telephone interviews with 1,042 adults during March 1985.

Source: Gallup Survey for the Religious Education Association of the United States and Canada

Most Americans give considerable thought to spiritual and existential matters, according to a 1985 survey assessing the extent to which they reflect on the worth and meaning of their lives and their relation to God.

A 67% majority reports giving "a lot" of thought to living a worthwhile life; an indication of the conscious value Americans place on virtue and self-esteem. Fifty-eight percent have thought a great deal about the more complex question of the meaning and value of their lives.

Regarding spiritual concerns, 59% say they have often reflected on their relation to God while nearly half, 47%, state they have thought a lot about faith development. These findings confirm the pervasiveness of active belief in God in the U.S. Correlational data show that reflection on the dimensions of faith relates positively to participation and activity within a church or synagogue.

MANY EXPERIENCE DIVINE GUIDANCE

Question:
Has God ever led or guided you in making any kind of decision in your life, or not?

	Yes %	No %	No opinion %
NATIONAL	83	13	4
Men	78	17	5
Women	86	9	5
18-29 years	77	20	3
30-49 years	84	11	5
50 and older	85	10	5
Whites	81	14	5
Blacks	91	6	3
Protestants	85	11	4
Catholics	78	17	5
Born-again Christians	93	5	2

Findings are based on telephone interviews with 1,013 adults nationwide during February 1986.

Source: Gallup Survey for the Christian Broadcasting Network, Inc.

A strong majority of U. S. adults who believe in God experience their faith pragmatically. Eighty-three percent say that God has guided them in making decisions, suggesting the pragmatic dimension of spirituality among Americans.

Reports of divine guidance are more frequent among women (86%) than men (78%), while nearly as many adults 18 to 29 (77%) say they receive such guidance as those 30 to 49 (84%) and 50 or older (85%). More blacks than whites agree by a margin of 91% to 81%.

Not surprisingly, born-again Christians (93%) are most inclined to say they God leads them in making life choices. Eighty-five percent of Protestants make this claim, considerably more than Catholics at 78%.

WHAT AMERICANS WOULD ASK GOD

Question:
Suppose you could ask God any *three* questions on this list. What would they be?

	National %
Will there ever be lasting world peace?	37
How can I be a better person?	33
What does the future hold for me and my family?	31
Will there ever be a cure for all diseases?	28
Why is there suffering in the world?	28
Is there life after death?	26
What is heaven like?	22
Will man ever love his fellow man?	21
Why is there evil in the world?	16
When will the world end?	16
Why was man created?	10
Don't know/ Don't believe in God	8

*Less than one percent.

Note: Percentages add to more than 100% due to multiple responses.

Findings are based on telephone interviews with 1,519 adults nationwide during October 1982.

Source: Gallup Survey for the Christian Broadcasting Network, Inc.

Given the chance to ask God three questions — some being obstacles to faith — Americans (37%) most frequently chose from a list of eleven whether there will ever be lasting world peace. A combined 44% would ask God why there is evil or suffering in the world, questions raised but never resolved by theologians and philosophers from antiquity to the present day.

One-third (33%) want to know how to become a better person. About as many (31%) would ask what the future holds for themselves and their families, while 28% express more global concerns about cures for disease and the cause of human suffering. A total of 48% would ask more timeless questions about life after death (26%) and the experience of heaven (22%). Twenty-one percent would ask about the capacity for love among humans, whereas 16% would put to God the questions of evil and when the world will end. Ten percent would ask why humans were created.

Among groups, older persons and Easterners are more likely to ask God about world peace. Women, whites and Midwesterners are disproportionately inclined to ask about being a better person. Higher levels of education and religious commitment relate positively among those who chose this question. Respondents who would like to know of the future for themselves and their families are more likely to be religious, non-white and Southern.

Episcopalians and Catholics indicate the greatest concern for world peace, while Jews and Lutherans most frequently ask why suffering exists. Methodists and Episcopalians emphasize the question of life after death, compared to Catholics, who want to know especially what heaven is like. Baptists and Presbyterians in particular cite the question of human love. Lutherans and Methodists show the highest interest in the apocalypse or the end of the world.

VII. Spiritual Development & Commitment

Despite signs of disaffection from organized religion, levels of spiritual development and commitment have remained steady and by some indicators, have risen over the past decade: evidence of pervasive expressions of faith in America, without necessary ties to church and synagogue.

In 1988 53% nationwide said that religion was "very important" in their lives, roughly that same percentage found in 1978 (52%). More particularly, 56% in 1984 said that "growing into a deeper relationship with God" was "very important," while in 1985, 51% understood the nature of faith to be a "relationship with God." By comparison only 19% saw faith in doctrinal terms as "a set of beliefs," and a tiny minority of 4% viewed faith in connection with church or synagogue membership.

Most Americans, on the other hand, say they have made a commitment to Jesus Christ, and the proportion of 66% cited in 1988 has risen from 60% in 1978, a six-point increase identical to the decade uptrend on belief in Christ's divinity, from 78% to 84%. The modest difference is significant because levels of commitment change slowly in the course of Gallup trend surveys. In addition a related survey conducted in 1983 showed 79% have "tried to follow the example of Jesus" to some extent at least.

In a 1984 study designed to measure spiritual commitment in America, a total of 84% reported that they try in earnest to practice their religious beliefs, while 72% agreed "completely" or "mostly" that their religious faith was the most important influence in their lives. Sixty-seven percent in the combined categories affirmed that they "constantly seek God's will through prayer."

Lifetime spiritual development clearly factors in the extent to which Americans are drawn to personal piety. Findings based on a 1988 survey showed that 82% of the U.S. population received religious training as children, although in 1987 on a ten-point scale, far fewer (18%) called themselves a "religious person" receiving a "ten" as a "perfect description." The percentage giving a "ten" increased steadily with age, which suggests a positive correlation between spiritual development and maturity.

In 1985 seven in ten adults (71%) said that their faith had changed significantly at some time in their lives, with those under 30 (80%) more likely to report such changes than persons 50 and older (62%). Related findings indicated changes in faith occur more frequently during times of stability than in crisis, confirming observations of many psychologists of religion that spiritual transformation may be innate to the adult life cycle.

RELIGION 'VERY IMPORTANT' TO 53% OF AMERICANS

Question:
How important would you say religion is in your own life—would you say it is very important, fairly important, or not very important?

	Very important %	Fairly important %	Not very important %	No opinion %
NATIONAL	53	31	15	1
Men	46	33	20	1
Women	61	29	10	*
18-29 years	44	36	20	*
30-49 years	50	34	15	1
50 and older	64	24	11	1
East	45	37	17	1
Midwest	54	32	13	1
South	63	26	10	1
West	48	31	21	*
College grads.	47	31	21	1
College inc.	51	33	15	1
H. S. grads	55	32	12	1
Not H. S. grads	58	27	14	1
Whites	51	33	15	1
Blacks	69	18	12	1
Hispanics	50	34	14	2
Protestants	62	28	9	1
Evangelicals	84	14	2	*
Non-evangelicals	40	38	21	1
Catholics	49	40	10	1

*Less than one percent.

Findings are based on personal and telephone interviews with 4,597 adults nationwide during 1988.

Source: Gallup Poll

The proportion of Americans who say religion is "very important" in their lives (53%) indicates the salience of religion in the U. S. and suggests the degree of religious value felt in personal terms among adults nationwide.

Gender and age play key roles in perceptions of religious significance, cited among women far more than men by (61% to 46%), and by persons 50 and older (64%) more frequently than adults 30 to 49 (50%) and 18 to 29 (44%). Similarly, religion is most likely to be very important among Southerners (63%), persons without high school diplomas (58%), and blacks (69%).

By religious groups more Protestants (62%) than Catholics (49%) say religion is very important, compared to the wide majority of Evangelicals (84%) and the lesser proportion of Non-evangelicals (40%).

Importance of Religion

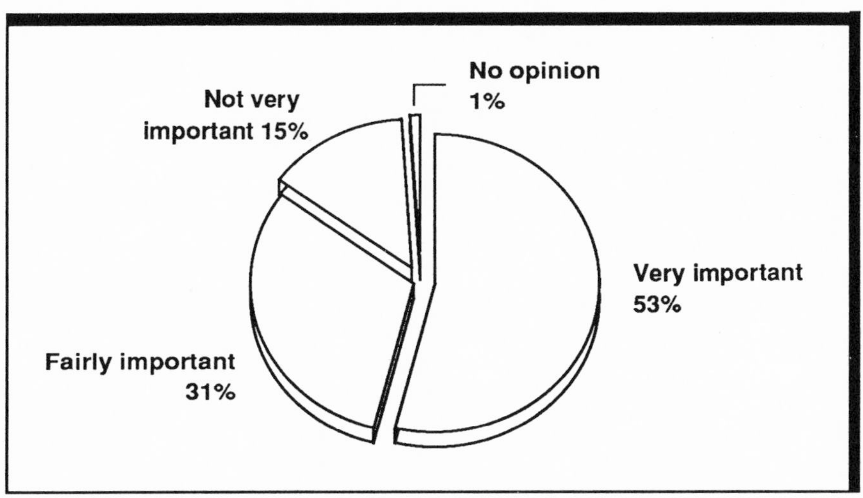

AMERICANS SEEK RELATIONSHIP WITH GOD

Question:
Please tell me whether . . . the following is very important, fairly important, not very important, or not at all important?

Growing into a deeper relationship with God

	Very important %	Fairly important %	Not very important %	Not at all important %	No opinion %
NATIONAL	56	26	10	6	2
Men	49	29	13	7	2
Women	62	24	7	5	2
18-29 years	50	30	13	4	3
30-49 years	55	27	9	8	1
50 and older	61	22	9	5	3
Protestants	67	22	7	3	1
Evangelicals	94	6	*	*	*
Non-evangelicals	45	32	12	8	3
Catholics	46	37	10	4	3

*Less than one percent.

Findings are based on personal interviews with 1,522 adults nationwide during June 1984.

Source: Gallup Survey for the Robert H. Schuller Ministries

In *Waiting for God,* Simone Weil wrote that God is the perfect friend who bridges an "infinite distance" between the divine and human realms. Most Americans share this understanding and experience of a God less transcendent than immanent: a total of 82% say that "growing into a deeper relationship with God" is important to them.

Relational spirituality is more pronounced among women than men by 86% to 78% who think it is important to grow closer to God. Conversely, 20% of men and 12% of women say such a relationship is not important.

The importance of knowing God rises with age. Sixty-one percent of adults 50 and older say it is "very important,"compared to 50% of persons 18 to 29 and 55% of those 30 to 49.

Sixty-seven percent of Protestants share this view, considerably more than Catholics (46%). A much wider gap is found, however, between Evangelicals (94%) and Non-evangelicals (45%).

STRIKING 66% CLAIM COMMITMENT TO JESUS CHRIST

Question:
Would you say you have made a commitment to Jesus Christ or not?

	Yes %	No %	No opinion %
NATIONAL	66	28	6
Men	60	34	6
Women	72	22	6
18-24 years	54	39	7
25-29 years	61	31	8
30-49 years	66	28	6
50 and older	73	22	5
East	58	35	7
Midwest	71	24	5
South	74	21	5
West	60	33	7
Protestants	77	18	5
Catholics	67	25	8
Churched	83	14	3
Unchurched	44	46	10

Findings are based on personal interviews with 2,556 adults nationwide during March 1988.

Source: Gallup Survey for the National Catholic Evangelization Association

Though varied in its many implications, commitment to Jesus Christ can best be summed in his call of Matthew to "follow me" (Matt. 9:9). Two in three American adults (66%) claim to have made such a commitment, while 28% say they have not.

Levels of commitment rise with age and are most pronounced among those over fifty (73%). More women than men have committed themselves to Christ by a margin of 72% to 60%. Southerners (74%) are more inclined to have done so than persons from the East (58%), the West (60%) and the Midwest (71%). Fewer Catholics (67%) than Protestants (77%) cite this commitment, a difference reflecting the concentration of Protestants who are evangelical and whose emphasis on spiritual rebirth includes an explicit christology.

A strong majority of churched respondents, 83%, say they have made a commitment to Christ; nearly twice as many as unchurched Americans at a substantial 44%.

AMERICANS' RELIGIOUS SELF ASSESSMENT

Question:
On a scale from 1 to 10, where 10 represents a description that is perfect for you, and 1 a description that is totally wrong for you, how well does the term, "a religious person," describe you?

—A Perfect Description—
(Choosing 10 on a 10-point scale)

NATIONAL	18 %
Men	14
Women	22
18-24 years	9
25-29 years	12
30-39 years	14
40-49 years	19
50-59 years	23
60 and over	27
Blacks	26
Hispanics	13
White Protestants	19
White Protestant evangelicals	35
White Protestant non-evangelicals	8
Black Protestant evangelicals	44
Black Protestant non-evangelicals	13
Catholics	15
White ethnic Catholics	15
White non-ethnic Catholics	14
Jews	13
Other	30
None	5

Results based on age and gender:

	Men %	Women %
18-29 years	10	11
30-49 years	13	19
50 and older	17	32

Findings are based on personal interviews with 4,244 adults nationwide during April/May 1987.

Source: Gallup Survey for *Times Mirror*

Older women are far more likely than older men to describe themselves as very religious, but younger men and women under 30 give about equal assessments of their levels of religiousness.

One-third (32%) of older women, 50 and over, rate themselves a "ten," twice the proportion of older men (17%) who do so. However, the 11% of younger women under 30 who choose "ten" statistically matches the percentage of men who do so.

Other highlights of the survey are:

- The percentage giving a "ten"— that is, who say that "a religious person" is a perfect description for themselves — increases steadily with age. Persons 60 years of age and older are three times as likely as those 18 to 24 to select a "ten" on the scale.

- More than four in ten (44%) black Protestant evangelicals pick the top position on the scale.

- Three in ten (31%) of those who are widowed choose a "ten."

MAJORITY OF AMERICANS RECEIVED EARLY RELIGIOUS TRAINING

Question:
Did you receive any religious training as a child?

	Yes %	No %
NATIONAL	82	18
Whites	83	17
Blacks	78	22
Hispanics	76	24
East	85	15
Midwest	81	19
South	81	19
West	83	17
Protestants	82	18
Catholics	90	10

Findings are based on personal interviews with 2,556 adults nationwide during March 1988.

Source: Gallup Survey for the National Catholic Evangelization Association

The extent of childhood religious training in the U.S. may account in part for the immense majorities who believe in God and give a religious preference. More than eight in ten nationwide (82%) received religious training as children, with greater numbers found among whites (83%), Easterners (85%) and Catholics (90%).

Although somewhat fewer blacks (78%), residents of the Bible Belt (81%), and Protestants (82%) report religious instruction while growing up, these are the traditional groups more likely to emphasize and practice religious priorities. The findings raise questions about the long-term effects of early religious training, which may not necessarily bear on spiritual commitments made during adult life. Related findings show that children of non-religious parents are more inclined to choose religious affiliations.

Majority Received Weekly Religious Training

To a question on types of early religious training, eight in ten (81%) said they were taught in Sunday school or weekly religious classes. More than one in four (28%) received instruction from their parents at home, and 22% attended religious or parochial school. One in nine (11%) took courses on religion in public or private schools.

BELIEVERS DEFINE FAITH

Question:
Which one of the following four statements comes closest to your own view of "faith"?

A set of beliefs
Membership in a church or synagogue
Finding meaning in life
A relationship with God

	Relationship with God %	Meaning in life %	Set of beliefs %	Church/ synagogue member %	Not meaningful %	No opinion %
NATIONAL	51	20	19	4	1	5
Men	44	21	24	3	2	6
Women	57	19	15	5	1	3
Protestants	59	17	16	4	*	4
Catholics	46	24	21	5	1	4
Jews	27	29	31	*	*	13
Other	48	16	24	2	2	8
None	20	34	33	*	5	8

*Less than one percent.

Findings are based on telephone interviews with 1,042 adults nationwide during March 1985.

Source: Gallup Survey for the Religious Education Association of the United States and Canada

More than half of all Americans (51%) feel that faith consists of a relationship with God. One in five (20%) views faith in terms of a meaningful life, and roughly the same proportion (19%) understands faith as a set of beliefs. A 4% minority sees faith as membership in a church or synagogue. One percent volunteered the opinion that faith was not meaningful to them.

Women are more likely than men to understand faith as a relationship with God, while more men define faith as a set of beliefs. Adults over 40 say faith is a relationship with God or church/synagogue membership more so than younger adults, who generally view faith as a set of beliefs or a context for making life meaningful.

The less educated are more prone to report that faith is a relationship with God or membership in a church or synagogue, whereas the college educated are inclined to identify faith with a set of beliefs.

Protestants, Southerners and church members more frequently say faith is a relationship with God. Among non-church members, there is less consensus on the definition of faith presented here; that is, a majority endorses none of the four possible definitions listed.

SPIRITUAL COMMITMENT STRONG IN U.S.

Question:
Please tell me for each of the following statements if you feel it is completely true, mostly true, mostly untrue or completely untrue.

	Completely true %	Mostly true %	Mostly untrue %	Completely untrue %	No opinion %
I believe in the divinity of Jesus Christ.	69	19	3	5	4
I believe that God loves me even though I may not always please him.	68	21	3	4	4
I wish my religious faith were stronger.	51	27	11	8	3
I believe in the full authority of the Bible.	51	26	9	9	5
I try hard to put my religious beliefs into practice in my relations with all people, including people of different races, religious attitudes and backgrounds.	49	35	7	5	4
I receive a great deal of comfort and support from my religious beliefs.	46	32	11	7	4
I constantly seek God's will through prayer.	36	31	19	11	3
My religious faith is the most important influence in my life.	34	38	17	8	3
I sometimes do things I want very much NOT to do because I believe it is the will of God.	23	26	19	23	9

Findings are based on personal interviews with 1,610 adults nationwide during April 1984.

Source: Gallup Survey for the Christian Broadcasting Network, Inc.

One in ten Americans (10%) can be called "highly spiritually committed," according to a scale developed by the Princeton Religion Research Center to measure levels of spiritual commitment nationwide.

The scale does not include religious involvement or participation items, since these do not necessarily measure spiritual commitment. Instead it determines levels of belief about God, the divinity of Jesus Christ, and the authority of the Bible. The scale also assesses the extent to which Americans seek a stronger faith and knowledge of God through prayer, and evaluates the practical and motivational dimensions of spirituality.

Respondents considered "highly spiritually committed" answered "completely true" to all nine statements. Results show a disproportionate number of women and persons with less than college training in this category.

Findings refer only to those in the sample who gave their broad religious preference as Christian, as there were too few non-Christians in the sample to provide projectible data.

SEVENTY-ONE PERCENT HAVE EXPERIENCED CHANGE IN FAITH

Question:
In terms of your own definition of "faith," would you say your faith changed significantly in the past 5 years, in the past 6-10 years, in the past 10-20 years, more than 20 years ago, or never?

		Age of Respondent			
	NATIONAL %	Under 30 %	30-39 %	40-49 %	50 and older %
Yes (total)	71	80	77	68	62
Within the past:					
5 years	31	54	30	27	14
6-10 years	20	22	28	17	15
10-20 years	16	10	24	14	16
More than 20 years ago	12	2	6	14	22
	79 %*	88 %*	88 %*	72 %*	67 %*
Never	29	20	23	32	38
Total	100 %	100 %	100 %	100 %	100 %

*Adds to more than total experiencing a change in faith due to multiple responses.

Findings are based on telephone interviews with1,042 adults nationwide during March 1985.

Source: Gallup Survey for the Religious Education Association of the United States and Canada

In order to gain some insight into the process of faith development, Gallup asked American adults about their perceived changes in faith. In a study that measures behavior at one point in time, it is not possible to measure the process of development directly. For this reason respondents were asked to reflect on the past and describe their associations with a significant change in faith. The results suggest the considerable extent to which adults understand faith to be a developmental process rather than a static state.

About seven in ten (71%) indicate their faith had changed significantly at some point. Most adults experiencing a change say it happened only once, although 5% report more than one change in faith.

Among those with a significant change, a majority answers that it took place within the past ten years. (Whether this is a true indication of the time of change or a function of respondents' ability to recall cannot be precisely determined.)

While few mention more than one such change, it appears that these experiences may occur several times in one's life. The large proportion within each age category reporting a change approximately ten years earlier, on average, supports this view.

STABILITY OFTEN ACCOMPANIES SPIRITUAL TRANSFORMATION

Question:
Would you say the [faith] change came at a time when your life was essentially stable or normal, or came at a time when your life was turbulent or chaotic?

(Based on those reporting change in faith)

	Stable/ normal %	Turbulent/ chaotic %	No opinion %
NATIONAL	59	40	1
Under 30 years	55	44	1
30-39 years	53	46	1
40-49 years	66	34	*
50 and older	64	34	2

*Less than one percent.

Findings are based on telephone interviews with 1,042 adults nationwide during March 1985.

Source: Gallup Survey for the Religious Education Association of the United States and Canada

Contrary to the view that spiritual transformation occurs on the heels of crises, a 59% majority reports a change in faith during a time of stability, while four in ten (40%) undergo change at a turbulent time. Adults over 40 are more likely than younger adults to experience change when their lives are stable.

Those indicating fairly recent changes in faith are more likely than others to report change during chaotic times. Not surprisingly, persons whose change led to a completely different faith are more likely than those with little change to say the transition came when their lives were turbulent.

To a related question, about equal proportions said that significant change resulted from much thought and discussion (46%) and from strong emotional experience (49%), with little difference between genders.

Times when faith change occurs

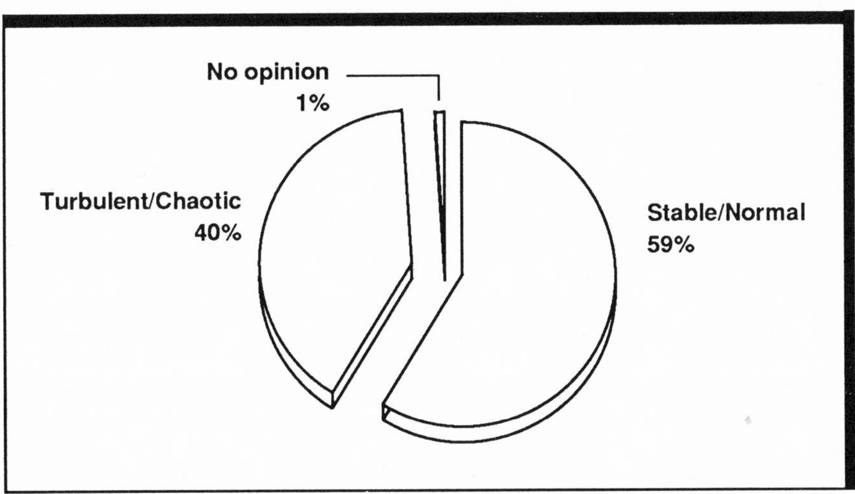

IMPORTANCE OF RELIGIOUS BELIEFS AMONG TEENS

Question:
How important are your religious beliefs: very important, fairly important, not too important, or not at all important?

	Very important %	Fairly important %	Not too important %	Not at all important %
NATIONAL	39	41	15	5
Young men	35	41	18	6
Young women	42	42	12	4
13-15 years	39	42	16	3
16-17 years	38	41	14	7
East	26	50	18	6
Midwest	31	48	17	4
South	62	32	6	0
West	30	38	21	10
Students:				
Above average	41	41	14	4
Average or below	36	42	16	5
Protestants	46	39	12	3
Catholics	28	51	19	1

Note: "No opinion" (one percent, nationally) omitted.

Findings are based on telephone interviews with 503 teens 13 to 17 nationwide during March 1987.

Source: Gallup Youth Poll

Assessing the importance of religious beliefs, most American teens attach some measure of significance to their faith, but in a related survey, half (49%) say religion is less important to them than to their parents.

The finding is not surprising. Adolescent struggle for identity marks the stage when teens discover and express what makes them unique as individuals and different from their parents. Psychologist Jean Piaget views this development in terms of a growing capacity to separate the ideal from the real, often resulting in disaffection from authority. Considering the added factor of secularization in American culture and churches, teens are becoming less inclined to cite spiritual priorities.

Nevertheless, 39% say their individual beliefs about religion are "very important," while 41% assert they are "fairly important." Only 15% think their beliefs are essentially insignificant. For 5%, faith is "not at all important."

Religious belief is more imporant among young women than young men and among above-average students, though age bears little effect on patterns of response. Southern youths are far more likely to stress the importance of faith than their counterparts; however, high proportions in the East and Midwest say it is fairly significant.

In addition 46% of Protestant teens indicate their beliefs are very important, as compared to 28% of Catholics, most of whom report a moderate degree of importance (51%).

Teens Compare Religious Priorities to Parents'

Only one-fourth of American teens (26%) think that faith matters more to them than their parents, and fewer feel it matters as much (24%). Large proportions nationwide say it is less important, with males slightly more prone to do so than females by 50% to 47%.

Teens 13 to 15 report less interest in religion than parents by 51%, somewhat more frequently than those 16 to 17 (45%). More adolescents from the East and students average or below respond similarly.

Better than half of Catholic youths (54%) believe religion affects them less than it does their parents. Forty-five percent of Protestant teens agree.

VIII. Trends

In the half century of scientific polling, rapid and dramatic social change has altered the nation's religious mood, despite the remarkable stability of beliefs and practices among Americans. While largely unchanged throughout survey history, mainline religious commitment was relatively low during the Depression years and the Second World War. But diverse movements such as Neo-orthodoxy, revival of the Social Gospel and a resurgence of fundamentalism sustained religious conservatives and liberals as well, until the American Right emerged in the 1950s.

Postwar recovery saw church and synagogue membership in 1947 at the highest level ever recorded by Gallup (76%). The ratio of Protestants to Catholics was far greater than today, with 69% of U. S. adults identifying themselves as Protestants and 20% as Catholics. In 1952, the year of Dwight D. Eisenhower's election, the trend peak of 75% nationwide found religion "very important." With the cold war well underway, "In God We Trust" became the national motto, the year after church and synagogue attendance reached a high of 49% in 1955, matched in 1958. And with American civil religion approaching religious nationalism, 69% in 1957 said the influence of religion on American life was increasing, compared to 36% in 1988.

The onset of the Vietnam War radically changed the mood of the 1950s. By 1965 deep disaffection with the social order had given rise to a counterculture that embraced Eastern mysticism and the politics of a new left. Public confidence in American institutions declined sharply in the wake of violence across campuses and inner cities, as the civil rights movement mounted and the Tet offensive shattered expectations of a military victory in Southeast Asia. Theologians reinvented Nietzsche's "death of God," but popular belief in God held firm at 97%. As for organized religion, however, membership, attendance, and the trend on the importance of religion fell, not only among Catholics but also among Protestants and Jews. National attendance dropped from 49% in 1958 to 42% in 1969, with the decline most pronounced among young adults (21 to 29 years), down fifteen points, and among Catholics, down eleven points. In 1962 31% nationwide felt that religion was losing influence on society, up seventeen points from 1957. By the end of the decade that percentage had climbed to 70%.

The early 1970s marked the breakdown of Americans' sense of national unity, and ushered in one of the lowest points in public morale. The devastating loss in Vietnam followed closely by Watergate intensified disillusion with government, and the effect on religious culture lasted well into the 1980s. Churches and synagogues suffered serious declines in membership and attendance, with churchgoing at 40%, down by nine percentage points from 1958. The downtrend traced almost entirely to falling attendance among Catholics, whose 1973 attendance rate of 55% fell from 71% ten years earlier. Furthermore, at the outset of the decade 75% suggested religion was losing impact; only 14% said it was gaining, almost exactly reversed from 1957. In mainline communities, as the distance grew between a liberal clergy and more conservative laity, both sides became reluctant to form a cohesive religious identity. Evangelical and revivalist churches, on the other hand, were advancing with new members toward the cultural mainstream.

In 1976 Jimmy Carter entered the Oval Office as a born-again Southern Baptist supported heavily by an evangelical Democratic constituency. By that year the slide of a decade and a half in religious involvement had leveled off. A marginal upturn to 42% occurred in weekly churchgoing, and membership steadied at 71%. The proportion of Americans reporting greater influence of religion grew to 44% and to 49% in 1985, more than triple the percentage recorded in 1970. Religious pluralism flourished, with a projected 10 million in 1976 involved in transcendental meditation, mysticism, yoga, or Eastern religions, 3 million in the charismatic movement, and 34% nationwide calling themselves born-again or evangelical Christians.

Key features of the religious climate lasted into the 1980s with moderate but notable differences. Following the 1980 election of born-again Ronald Reagan, optimism among conservatives reflected a discernable movement to the right in statements of faith among many major religious bodies. Attendance and membership levels remained stable, along with the proportion of 56% saying religion is "very important." But relocations away from liberal and moderate Protestant churches had drained their numbers during years of growth among Catholics, Southern Baptists, Latter-day Saints and Pentecostals. Evangelical affiliation nationwide held steady into 1988 (33%). Nevertheless, public confidence in organized religion has dropped to 59%, compared to 66% in 1985. With the trend on belief in God unchanged (94%), the 1988 membership figure reached a low point of 65% — evidence of ongoing religious relocation. Between 1986 and 1988 the proportion reporting increased influence of religion dropped from 48% to 36%.

By the time yet another born-again Christian George Bush won the presidency, the religious mood of the mid-1970s had given way to the climate of ambivalence that attends social transition and cultural change. Given the prevalence of religious privacy in America today, his inaugural call for voluntary public virtue and civil religious values may reflect a broad but diffuse base of support for the nation's spiritual regeneration in the decade ahead.

LITTLE CHANGE IN RELIGIOUS PREFERENCES

Question:

What is your religious preference — Protestant, Roman Catholic, Jewish, Mormon, or an Orthodox Church such as the Greek or Russian Orthodox Church?

	Protestant %	Catholic %	Jewish %	Other %	None %
1988	56	28	2	4	10
1987	57	28	2	4	9
1986	58	27	2	4	9
1985	57	28	2	4	9
1984	57	28	2	4	9
1983	56	29	2	4	9
1982	57	29	2	4	8
1981	59	28	2	4	7
1980	61	28	2	2	7
1979	59	29	2	2	8
1977-78	60	29	2	1	8
1976	61	27	2	4	6
1975	62	27	2	4	6
1974	60	27	2	5	6
By Five -Year Periods					
1972	63	26	2	4	5
1967	67	25	3	3	2
1962	70	23	3	2	2
1957	66	26	2	4	5
1952	67	25	4	1	2
1947	69	20	5	1	6

Note: Results for some years do not add up to 100% because of rounding.

Latest findings are based on personal and telephone interviews with 15,460 adults nationwide during 1988.

Source: Gallup Poll

The 1988 Gallup audit indicates little change in recent years in the relative strength of major faiths in this country, with 56% in the latest series of surveys giving their religious preference as Protestant, 28% Roman Catholic, 2% Jewish, and 2% Mormon.

Since 1947 the proportion of Catholics in America has increased from 20% to 28% in 1988. Conversely, the figure for Protestants has declined from 69% in 1947 to 56% today. The proportion of Jews has dropped from 5% in 1947 to 2% in the 1970s and 1980s.

The percentage giving no religious preference (10%) closely matches that recorded in the five previous years, but since 1967 has risen gradually and is significantly higher today than the 2% recorded that year.

'MAINLINE' AFFLIATION DOWN

Question:
What is your religious preference?

	Baptist %	Methodist %	Lutheran %	Presbyterian %	Episcopalian %
1988	20	10	6	4	2
1987	20	9	6	3	2
1986	20	9	5	2	2
1985	20	10	6	2	2
1984	20	9	7	2	3
1983	21	10	7	3	2
1982	19	10	6	4	2
1981	19	10	6	4	2
1980	19	10	6	4	2
1979	19	11	6	4	2
1978	19	11	6	4	2
1976	21	11	7	5	3
1975	20	11	7	5	3
1974	21	14	7	6	3
1969	20	14	7	6	3
1967	21	14	7	6	3

Latest findings are based on personal and telephone interviews with 15,460 adults nationwide during 1988.

Source: Gallup Poll

The percentage of adults who state a preference for mainline Protestant denominations continues to fall below the levels recorded in the 1960s and early and mid-1970s. In the latest audit 20% chose a Baptist church, 10% a Methodist, 6% Lutheran, 4% Presbyterian and 2% Episcopalian.

The percentage of adults who give their denominational preference as Methodist, Lutheran, Presbyterian and Episcopalian has levelled off in the last few years after sharp declines in the 1970s and 1960s.

While those who give their preference as Baptist have shown little change over the two decades measured, the proportions in three of the four mainline churches — Methodist, Presbyterian and Episcopalian — have fallen off by one-third. The decline has been less precipitous among Lutherans.

Figures represent *preference* as distinguished from *membership*.

MEMBERSHIP REACHES LOWEST POINT IN SURVEY HISTORY

Question:
Do you happen to be a member of a church or synagogue?

	Yes %
1988	*65
1987	69
1986	69
1985	71
1984	68
1983	69
1982	67
1981	68
1980	69
1979	68
1978	68
1977	70
1976	71
1975	71
1965	73
1952	73
1947	**76
1944	75
1942	75
1940	72
1939	72
1938	73
1937	73

** High Point
* Low Point

Latest findings are based on interviews with 4,597 adults nationwide during 1988.

Source: Gallup Poll

Two thirds of U. S. adults (65%) say they are members of a church or synagogue, as determined by the 1988 Gallup audit.

The highest figure in the half-century trend occurred in 1947 when 76% said they were church or synagogue members. Today's percentage is the lowest recorded.

In 1988, as in past years, a higher percentage of women than men reported being church members. While membership increases progressively with age, education does not appear to be a major factor. But sharp differences are found by region, with Southerners most likely and Westerners least likely to be members.

It is important to bear in mind that the membership figures are self-classifications, representing the percentages of people who say they are members of a church or synagogue, and thus may include some who are not actually on the rolls of a local church. It should also be noted that adherents of certain churches — for example, the Roman Catholic and Eastern Orthodox Churches — are considered members at birth.

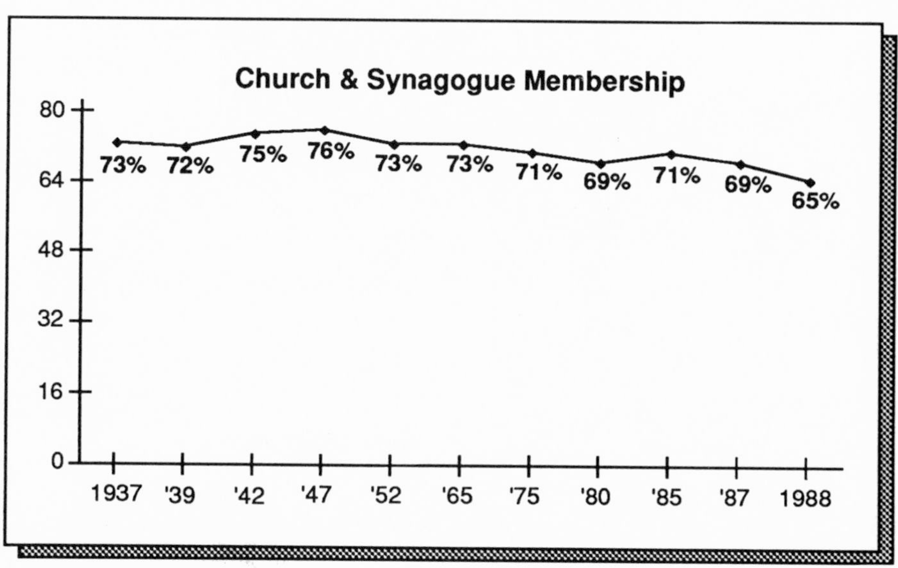

ATTENDANCE STEADY AT 42% NATIONWIDE

Question:
Did you, yourself, happen to attend church or synagogue in the last seven days?

	Yes %
1988	42
1987	40
1986	40
1985	42
1984	40
1983	40
1982	41
1981	41
1980	40
1979	40
1978	41
1977	41
1972	40
1969	42
1967	43
1962	46
1958	**49
1957	47
1955	**49
1954	46
1950	39
1940	*37
1939	41

** HighPoints
* Low Point

Latest findings are based on interviews with 2,041 adults nationwide during 1988.

Source: Gallup Poll

In a typical week of 1988, four adults in every ten (42%) attended church or synagogue, a figure that has remained remarkably constant since 1969, following a decline from the high point of 49% recorded in 1955 and 1958.

The trend reached its nadir of 37% in 1940, as the Depression neared its end prior to U. S. involvement in the Second World War. A rift between fundamentalists and modernists had divided Protestants, whose more liberal factions joined Catholics and Jews in social reforms and secular community life, but far less participation in organized religion.

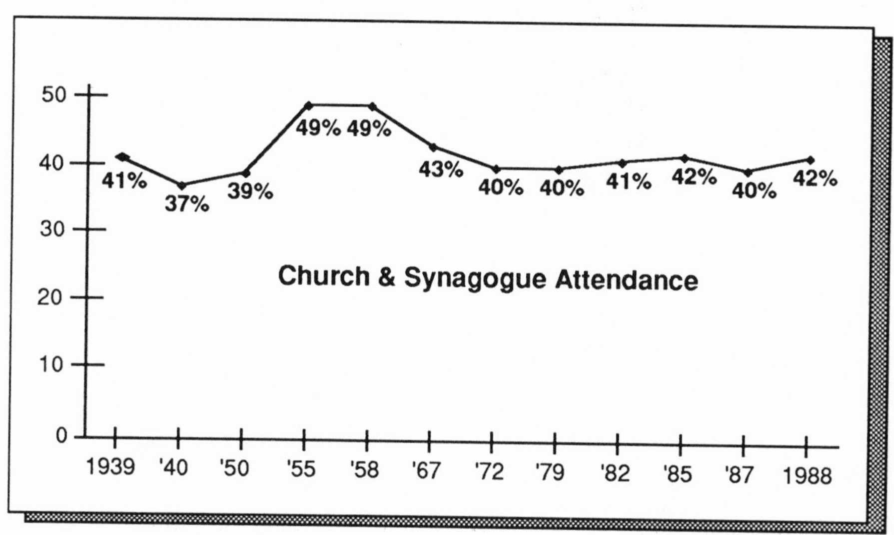

BELIEF IN GOD STAYS CONSTANT

Question:
Do you believe in God or a universal spirit?

	Yes %
1986	94
1981	95
1976	94
1975	94
1969	98
1967	97
1965	97
1959	97
1954	96
1953	98
1952	99
1947	94
1944	96

Latest findings are based on telephone interviews with 1,013 adults nationwide during February 1986.

Source: Gallup Survey for the Christian Broadcasting Network, Inc.

Ninety-four percent of all Americans in 1986 said they believe in God or a universal spirit, a proportion remarkably constant during nearly four decades of scientific polling. The trend shows little statistical change from 1944, with the highest level in 1952 at 99%.

IMPORTANCE OF RELIGION ON DOWNTREND SINCE 1950s

Question:
How important would you say religion is in your life — very important, fairly important, or not very important?

	Very important %	Fairly important %	Not very important %
1988	53	31	15
1987	53	32	14
1986	55	30	14
1985	55	31	13
1984	56	30	13
1983	56	30	13
1982	56	30	13
1981	56	29	14
1980	55	31	13
1978	52	32	14
1965	70	22	7
1952	75	20	5

Note: "No opinion" omitted.

Latest findings are based on interviews with 4,597 adults nationwide during 1988.

Source: Gallup Poll

A majority of Americans, 53%, consider religion very important in their lives, with women, older persons, Southerners, blacks and Southern Baptists most likely to give this response.

Although there has been little change in recent years in the proportion who say religion is very important to them, the current figure is 22 points lower than in 1952, when 75% cited its significance. That percentage dropped to 52% in 1978 and has since remained stable, with a slight uptrend during the 1980s.

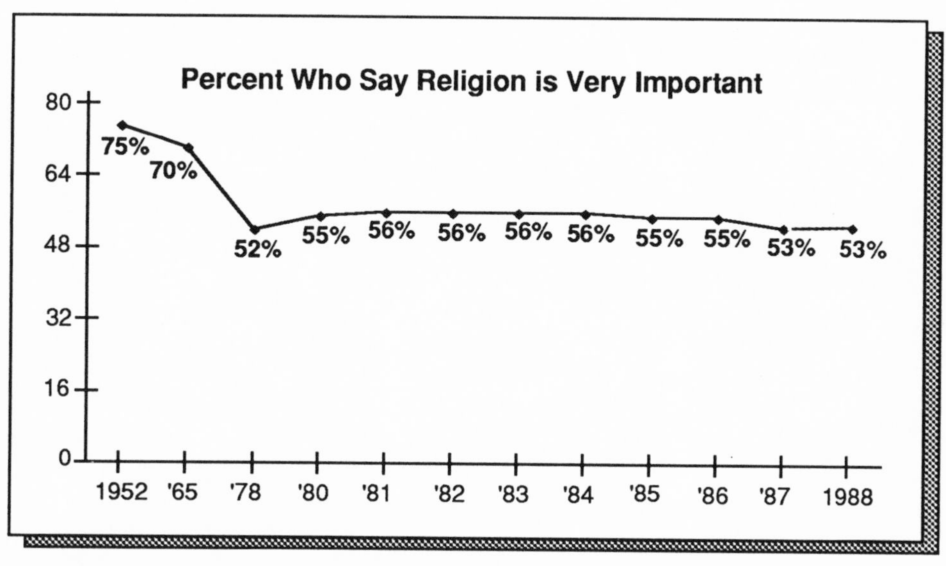

RELIGION'S INFLUENCE EBBS

Question:
At the present time, do you think religion as a whole is increasing its influence on American life or losing its influence?

	Increasing %	Losing %
1988	36	49
1986	48	39
1985	49	39
1984	42	39
1983	44	42
1981	38	46
1980	35	46
1978	37	48
1977	36	45
1976	44	45
1975	39	51
1974	31	56
1970	14	75
1969	14	70
1968	18	67
1967	23	57
1965	33	45
1962	45	31
1957	69	14

Latest findings are based on telephone interviews with 1,003 adults nationwide during March 1988.

Source: Gallup Poll

The number who think religion is losing its influence in America has grown sharply, from 39% in 1986 to 49% in 1988. Thirty-six percent say the influence of religion is growing, while 6% see little change. These findings suggest the current climate of religious disaffection seen also in downtrends in churchgoing and the influence and importance of religion in the U.S.

Of those who think religion's influence is decreasing, the sharpest change occurred between the (September) 1986 and the (March) 1988 surveys among younger adults and Protestants.

When this index was begun in 1957, 69% felt religion was gaining influence on American life, while far fewer, 14%, disagreed. By 1969 the figures were reversed. Between 1969 and 1985, however, a steady upturn was found among those reporting increased religious influence in America. Since 1986 the trend has reversed again.

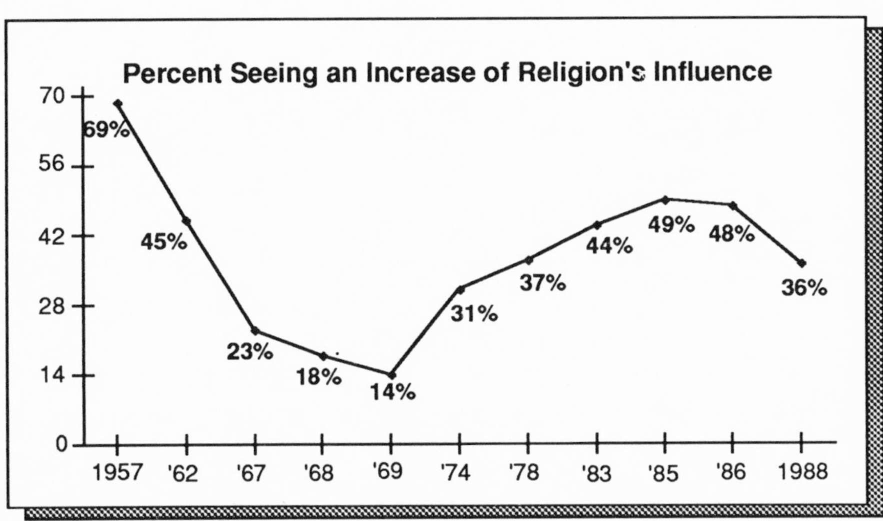

FEWER SAY RELIGION CAN ANSWER PROBLEMS

Question:
Do you believe that religion can answer all or most of today's problems, or that religion is largely old-fashioned and out of date?

	Can answer %	Out of date %	No opinion %
1988	57	20	23
1986	57	23	20
1985	61	22	17
1984	56	21	23
1982	60	22	18
1981	65	15	20
1974	62	20	18
1957	81	7	12

Latest findings are based on telephone interviews of 1,003 adults nationwide during March 1988.

Source: Gallup Poll

A majority of Americans (57%) believe that religion can answer all or most of today's problems, while 20% disagree and another 23% are undecided. The 1988 figure on religious relevance statistically matches the 1986 finding, but represents a marginal decline from 61% recorded in 1985. The 1988 level, however, dropped far below the peak figure of 1957 when 81% said religion can redress world dilemmas.

Most inclined to affirm religious solutions are women, blacks, persons 50 and older, Southerners and Evangelicals.

THIRD OF AMERICANS HAVE HAD POWERFUL RELIGIOUS AWAKENING

Questions:

Would you say you have ever had a religious or mystical experience, that is, a moment of sudden insight or awakening?

	Yes %
1988	33
1983	37
1978	35
1976	31
1962	20

Have you ever had what you consider to be an important religious experience that reinforced your faith?

	Yes %
1985	38

Have you ever had a religious experience — this is a particularly powerful insight or awakening that changed that direction of your life, or not?

	Yes %
1982	34
1981	34
1980	30
1978	34

Was this a sudden experience or a more gradual one? (Asked of those who had such an experience.)

	Sudden %	More Gradual %	Don't know %
1978	40	59	1

Note: The "no opinion" category averages 3% for all surveys.

Latest findings are based on personal interviews with 2,556 adults nationwide during March 1988.

Source: Gallup Survey for the National Catholic Evangelization Association

One-third of Americans have had what could be described as a "religious experience" — a particularly powerful religious insight or awakening, according to a recent national survey on *The Unchurched American*. This is roughly the same proportion as recorded in eight earlier surveys going back to 1976, in which similar questions were asked.

The religious experience is one of the least explored, yet most fascinating aspects of the spiritual life of Americans, sometimes described as an other-worldly feeling of union with God or a universal spirit. William James made one of the earliest attempts to study this phenomenon in his classic, *The Varieties of Religious Experience*, published in 1901. Now, by means of national scientific surveys, it is possible to take a more systematic approach to this aspect of religion.

The Gallup Poll first explored religious experience in 1962, one of the earliest national surveys on this topic. In that survey 20% said they had had a religious experience, up to 31% in 1976. Later Gallup surveys have recorded similar results, with percentages ranging between 30% and 38%. Some of the differences in the percentages may be due to wording variations.

Many who have a religious experience are able to recreate details, even the exact date of the occurrence. Such an experience often appears to have a profound effect on the outlook and direction of a person's life. Many recount experiences at times of crises, others in answer to prayers. Survey evidence also reveals that these experiences are more often gradual than sudden.

One of the most interesting aspects of these phenomena is that they happen to the non-churched and the non-religious as well as to persons who attend church regularly or who say religion plays an important role in their lives.

These experiences tend to fall into the following six general categories:

1. An "other-worldly" feeling of union with a Divine Being, carrying with it the conviction of the forgiveness of sins and salvation.
2. Dramatic spiritual awakening related to natural events such as sunsets or starry nights.
3. Experiences related to healing.
4. Experiences involving visions, voices and dreams.
5. A sudden insight and turning to God in a moment of crisis (death or near-death, war, car accident, etc.).
6. Unable to describe experience.

RELIGIOUS GIVING SETS RECORD HIGH

Question:
How much have Americans given to religious organizations?

	Amount (Billions)
1987	$43.61
1986	41.68
1985	37.46
1984	35.43
1983	31.61
1982	28.06
1981	25.05
1980	20.23
1979	20.17
1978	18.35
1977	16.98
1976	14.18
1975	12.81
1974	11.84
1973	10.53
1972	10.19
1971	10.07
1970	9.34

Source: *GIVING USA*, a publication of the American Association of Fund-Raising Council Trust for Philanthropy

Religious organizations were the major recipients of all donations in 1987, receiving $43.61 billion or 46.5% of total giving in America, and reflecting a steady increase since 1970.

According to the AAFRC Trust for Philanthropy, giving to religion has been nearly half of total philanthropy every year and varies by only a few points up or down, depending mostly on the volume and value of large gifts and bequests to other philanthropic categories such as education, health and culture.

The AAFRC Trust's estimate for total giving to religion is based on reports it receives from religious organizations. Those organizations are asked how much contributions were up or down in the previous year. The data are then weighted and averaged to arrive at an overall percentage change from the previous year.

IX. Glossary

Absolution: In the Catholic sacrament of penance, the forgiveness of sins.

Accommodation: Application of certain passages from the Hebrew Bible to the New Testament, to which they have no apparent historical reference. In a broader sense, adaptation of belief, doctrine or morality to cultural change or scientific discovery.

Agnostic: From the Greek word for "not know," signifying the unknown or unknowable. The term was coined by Thomas Henry Huxley in an 1889 essay claiming a person cannot have knowledge of phenomena that are not apprehended by the senses. The agnostic neither affirms nor denies the existence of God or the unseen world, but declares that the evidences for belief are inconclusive.

Alienation: In theological discourse, a term used chiefly by existentialists to explain the concept of sin. In classical theology, sin was held to be the state of being turned away from God (*aversio a Deo*); as described today, estranged.

Allah: The general name for God among Arabic speaking people.

Amen: A Hebrew word meaning "to trust," showing assent to an oath, acceptance of an utterance, or approval of a course of action. Jesus used the word, and early Christians used it regularly to mean "yes."

Animism: The belief that animals, plants, places and people have souls or spirits which are physical, not metaphysical, and are often equated with the breath, blood, name or shadow of the object or creature.

Annunciation: The announcement by an angel Gabriel to Mary that she will have a son, as reported in Luke 1:26-35.

Apocalypticism: Apocalyptic literature is characterized by most or all of the following traits. (1) Its perspective is of a definitive end time, the transition from this historical age into a world to come. (2) It adopts the literary forms of prophecy and asserts that the present and imminent end time with which it is concerned was predicted long ago. (3) Its vehicle of communication is an imitation of prophetic vision both complex and allegorical. (4) It proliferates in symbolism and esoteric imagery. (5) It derives especially from Persian and Hellenistic literary traditions. The NT church was formed during the dominance of the apocalyptic mentality.

Apocrypha: A term deriving from the Greek word *apokryphos*, meaning "hidden," to refer especially to a particular collection of writings, many of which are accepted as canonical scripture by Roman Catholics and other Christians. Originally, when applied to writings, the term denoted that their content was either not to be made available to the general public or else was obscure and difficult to understand. The word came to be used to designate noncanonical biblical texts.

Apologetics: The branch of theology concerned with a reasoned defense of the Christian religion and proofs for the existence of God.

Apostate: A person who by choice separates from a body to which he or she belongs, whether that be a national or religious community.

Ark of The Covenant: A box made of acacia wood overlaid with gold and crowned with two golden cherubim bending over the cover or "mercy seat," which ancient Israelis believed to have been God's throne or footstool. It is said to have contained the two tablets of the law that Moses brought down from Horeb.

Armageddon: The geographic place name (in Hebrew), apparently meaning "mountain of Megiddo," though there is no certainty that this is what is intended in the sole biblical reference to Armageddon (Rev. 16:16). In that verse the place is the meeting point of the kings of the world who gather for apocalyptic judgment dispensed by God.

Astrology: Divination and analysis of events and personalities through the study of celestial movement, not distinguished from astronomy until the sixteenth and seventeenth centuries with the rise of modern scientific inquiry.

Atheism: The denial that any reality is designated by what the religions call "God."

Atonement: A central doctrine in biblical theology and the formulation of the Christian message. In its essence the Anglo-Saxon word (*at-one-ment*, that is, making "at one") refers to the restoration of harmonious relations between God and humankind.

Attrition: In Catholic theology, a preparation for the grace of love that brings forth contrition, or genuine sorrow for sin.

Baptism: A sacrament of initiation into the Christian Church by immersion or sprinkling of water symgbolizing birth in Christ.

Beatitudes: The series of statements of Jesus reported in Matt. 5:1-12 and Luke 6:20-23, in which he pronounces the benefits bestowed by God on the faithful.

Benediction: A blessing, in Protestant churches, as parting prayer or invocation of the Lord at the end of a worship service. In the Roman Catholic Church, it communicates divine powers by purifying or blotting out sins of omission and the temporal punishment for sins.

Biblical Criticism: Scholarly determination of authenticity, authorship, dates and historical milieu of biblical texts.

Biblical Realism: The social and ethical outlook of Neo-Orthodox social commentators such as Reinhold Niebuhr (1892-1971), who stressed the tragic dimension of history occasioned by original sin, and the call of God for people to act responsibly to limit evil and promote human good.

Biblical Theology: A method of study for approaching theology from a biblical rather than a philosophical point of view and for seeking an understanding of the text consistent with what it might have meant to its first readers.

Bioethics: A field of applied ethics developed over the past quarter century that deals with the capability to keep terminally ill (or injured) patients alive with elaborate life support systems and to transplant vital organs, as well as the knowledge that makes these activities possible. Bioethics includes medical activities, but is a larger field of concern relating to questions about manipulation of the DNA chain or genetic reproduction.

Black Theology: A contemporary theological movement of diverse viewpoints that arose among black religious leaders in the United States during the 1960s. With a history originating in the nineteenth- century struggle against slavery, black theologians view the struggle of American blacks for equality and justice as equivalent to Moses calling Israel out of Egyptian slavery, or to Jesus' liberation from the bondage of sin. Major proponents include Martin Luther King, Jr., Marcus Garvey and James Cone.

B'nai B'rith: The oldest and largest Jewish fraternal organization, founded in 1843, whose programs include communal service, social action and educational programs.

Book of Common Prayer: The authorized liturgical service book of the Church of England used also by all churches in the worldwide Anglican communion.

Book of Mormon: A book published in 1830 by Joseph Smith (1805-1844), founder of the Church of Jesus Christ of Latter-Day Saints or Mormons, and accepted as divinely inspired by that group.

Born Again: A popular phrase for the experience of conversion or turning away from sin and a drawing closer to God through Christ. The phrase is based on Jesus' word to Nicodemus that he must be "born again" (John 3:3).

Canon: The term transliterates a Greek word meaning "rule," originally a carpenter's measuring stick. An older Hebrew word with virtually the same spelling designated a measuring reed about nine feet long. Since the fourteenth century the term has come to be used in reference to that collection of books recognized by the church as its authority but most often designated simply as the Bible.

Canon Law: In the polity of the Roman Catholic Church, a body of legal regulations that are no longer exercised by the ecclesiastical hierarchy. Canon law deals with the relations of church and state, the legal rights of heretics, the church's jurisdiction over its priests and their exclusion from secular legal sanctions, and other matters over which the Church has lost control since the sixteenth century.

Casuistry: In theology, the bearing of general moral principles upon specific and unique cases—for example, killing or lying. The obligatory practice of confession of sin in the late middle ages made the study of casuistry especially imperative in the training of priests.

Catechisms: Writings used to teach the basic content of the Christian faith.

Categorical Imperative: Ethical teaching of Immanuel Kant (1724-1804) that an action has worth only if it is done from a sense of duty; *i.e.*, in obedience to moral law. It is formulated thus: "I ought never to act except in such a way that I can also will that my maxim should become a universal law."

Catholic Reformation: A move toward renewal and reform within Roman Catholicism dominated, by reactions to sixteenth-century Protestantism.

Charismatics: Christians who profess to have received the baptism or fullness of the Holy Spirit. It is usually accompanied or followed by conferring on the believer one of the gifts (charismata) of the Spirit described in the Pauline Epistles. Experienced in wide ranges of the church, it is associated with the charismatic movement, charismatic renewal, or Neo-Pentecostalism.

Christology: The branch of theology that deals systematically with the person and acts of Jesus Christ.

Civil Religion: A term denoting the melding of national and religious goals. Christian civil religion emerged when Constantine's Edict of Milan (313) established a partnership between church and state. Civil religion emerged in America with the Puritans, who thought of themselves as chosen by God to establish a new Israel where magistrate and minister would work hand in hand. Sidney E. Mead in 1963 said the identification of American churches with nationalism was as complete as had ever been known in Christendom. However, the church-state consensus of religiosity and patriotism was denounced theologically in the Neo-orthodoxy of Karl Barth (1886-1968) and was shaken by the defeat of the U.S. in Viet Nam.

Contemplative Life: The name given to a life devoted mostly to prayer and devotional exercises—particularly the divine office, meditation, silence and fasting.

Conversion: To be changed inwardly, to turn to God, to be reborn; understood as a shift from sin to repentance and faith.

Convocation: From the Latin word *convocatio,* for "calling together," an ecclesiastical group called together to discuss church affairs.

Corrupt Text: A term used in the textual study of the Bible to refer to a passage that has been modified in the transmission of the text to express a theological viewpoint or to harmonize it with a parallel passage.

Cosmology: Metaphysical speculation or understanding of the origin and structure of the universe.

Covenant: A Hebrew term meaning "a binding pact" or "a compact," used for alliances between people; for example, Abraham and the Amorites (Gen. 14:13) and Israel and the Canaanites (Exod. 23:32). All such covenants are conditional, being predicated on stipulated terms at the time of ratification. In cases of covenants between God and humans, the stipulations are divine, and people have a choice of accepting or rejecting but not offering alternative conditions. Jesus spoke of the wine at the institution of the Lord's Supper as being a (new) covenant in his blood, poured out for the forgiveness of sins (Matt. 26:28).

Creation: In biblical terms, the divine action that called the universe into existence and ensures its continuity.

Creationism: In popular terms, the belief that all living creatures were brought into being within the last 10,000 years. Theologically, the doctrine that God creates each soul out of nothing (*ex nihilo*) and implants the soul in the body at birth or conception.

Creeds/Credo: A brief statement of faith, chiefly with a liturgical function.

Crucifixion: A form of execution by fastening the condemned to two crossed beams. Ezra 6:11 suggests that crucifixion was a practice of the Persians; the Greeks did not use it. Roman law ordered it for slaves, malefactors, religious and political agitators, murderers, pirates and others who had no civil rights. Jesus, as a seditionist, might be crucified but Paul, a Roman citizen, could not be.

Dead Sea Scrolls: Six hundred manuscripts discovered by chance in 1947 in a cave overlooking the Dead Sea, dating from the end of the second century B.C.E. to the mid-first century C.E. Called the Qumran, the scrolls contain biblicàl texts, commentary and liturgical texts.

Death of God Theology: A movement that flourished in the U.S. between 1960 and 1970. *The Death of God* by Gabriel Vahanian drew attention to the absence of the "God hypothesis" in the twentieth century and the fact that all educated people do not invoke God as an explanation of events once ascribed to God's agency (sickness and health, good harvests, natural disasters, etc.). The death of God theology was an attempt to restate Christian theology without a doctrine of God.

Decalogue: The Ten Commandments summarizing the agreement between Jehovah and the Hebrew people at Mount Sinai, known in Hebrew as the ten words or ten statements and appearing in slightly differing versions in Exod. 20 and Deut. 5.

Deism: From the Latin word *deus* ("god"), the term is used for a distinct belief about God and for a movement of the late seventeenth and eighteenth centuries reflecting the religious views of the Enlightenment. Deism teaches that God created the world but does not providentially guide or supernaturally intervene in nature or in human affairs. It is a belief of Deism that the world's intelligible order is demonstrable proof of an intelligent creator and that reason alone is sufficient to deduce all that is necessary to know about God's nature and purpose.

Determinism: The view that all human actions are necessary effects of earlier events that "caused" them. Determinism is most discussed *vis à vis* free will.

Diaspora: The scattered members of a religious community separated from the main body of fellow believers either in the same country or in another country. The concept of a diaspora arose after 722 B.C.E. when Israel fell to Assyria, and in 586 B.C.E. when Judah was conquered by Babylonia and many Jews were carried away into exile.

Diocese: A territorial division of the Roman Catholic, Episcopal (Anglican), and old Catholic churches, presided over by a bishop.

Doctrine: From the Latin *doctrina*, meaning "teaching," the term refers to the formulation or systematization of religious beliefs; for example, the doctrine of the Trinity.

Dogma: From the Greek verb *dokein*, "to seem good," dogma is a doctrine which has been given authoritative status by the church.

Druze: An offshoot of the Ismailiyya sect of the Shi'ite branch of Islam (Shi'ism). The movement began around 1000 C.E. during the reign of al-Hakin, who is worshipped and thought to be the incarnation of the Creator. The Druze teach the reincarnation of souls, and believe al-Hakin will return.

Ecclesiology: That branch of theology dealing systematically with the biblical and traditional teachings concerning the church.

Ecumenical Movement: The movement toward greater visible unity and cooperation among all Christian churches.

Election: The belief that God chooses people and groups to be special agents of God's saving purposes. Election (also called predestination in Christian theology) is central to the Hebrew Bible with its emphasis on Israel as the chosen people, and is basic to NT attempts to understand the unmerited grace of God.

Eschatology: That branch of theology that deals with "last things": death, judgment, heaven, hell, the final destinies of individuals and of the cosmos.

Ethics: Generally, reflection on the moral significance of human action and conduct or ways of life. It has come to mean reflection on values and morality, and may also be called moral philosophy or moral theology.

Eucharist: The chief sacrament of the Christian church, derived from the Last Supper, celebrated by Jesus the evening before his crucifixion. Believers eat the bread and drink of the cup in remembrance of him.

Evangelicalism: Derived from the Greek NT *euangelion,* meaning the "Gospel," interpreted as the good news of the promise of salvation to all who have faith in Jesus Christ. From the time of Martin Luther (1483-1546), the term has been used of Protestants to mean adherence to Christ and the Bible as the only rule of faith and practice in the church. In America, Evangelicalism became the name for the revivalism that characterized American Reformed and free-church Protestantism (especially Baptists and sectarians), from the time of Jonathan Edwards (1703-58) to Billy Sunday and Billy Graham in the twentieth century. This movement has varied widely from Lutheran Christianity in that it has stressed religious experience and conscious conversion.

Exegesis: The philological and historical interpretation of ancient texts, especially biblical texts, with the effort to reconstruct the original text on the basis of manuscript tradition (textual criticism) and analysis of content (historical criticism).

Exile: That period between the years 597 and 538 B.C.E. in which citizens of Jerusalem and Judea were forced to live in Babylon (cf. 2 Kings 24:18-25:30 and Jer. 52:1-34).

Extrasensory Perception (ESP): Sometimes called parapsychology, the term includes: telepathy, knowledge of anothers' thoughts; clairvoyance; supernormal awareness of objects or events; precognition, knowledge of future events; and psychokinesis, the ability to will the movement of an object without touching it. The Bible describes events in these categories narrated as dreams, healings and premonitions or prophecies of the future.

Faith: A believer's attitude toward God which involves the whole person; not only belief or intellectual assent, but also the will and experience.

Feminist Theology: Whether developed by women or men, a feminist theology is one based on the experience of women and seeks to promote equality between the sexes and among all people. It begins with the understanding that sexism, the historic domination of men over women, is a fundamental expression of evil and seeks a reconstruction of systems of meaning and action that devalue or negate the female.

Fideism: The doctrine that humanity is saved by faith alone.

Free Churches: Churches without government or external ecclesiastical control.

Friends, Society of (Quakers): A mystical reform movement in English Protestantism that grew out of the "inner light" experiences and preaching of George Fox (1624-91) and other itinerant preachers in the mid-seventeenth century. Quakers uphold the authority of divine inner revelation and practice spontaneous, unprogrammed group worship without ordained leadership.

Fundamentalism: A term derived from a series of twelve booklets on conservative Protestant Christian theology published and mailed to three million people over the years 1910-15 by two wealthy Los Angeles laymen, Lyman and Milton Stewart. Entitled *The Fundamentals,* these works attacked naturalism as the basis of contemporary liberal theology and expounded "the five fundamentals" adopted by the General Assembly of the Presbyterian Church in the U.S. in 1910. These included: the inerrancy of scriptures; the deity and virgin birth of Jesus Christ; the substitutinary theory of atonement (that Christ's death atoned for human sin); the physical resurrection of Christ; and Christ's miracles. Conservatives have added original sin, justification by faith, the Second Coming and a literal heaven and hell. An interdenominational phenomenon, fundamentalism grew out of nineteenth century American revivalism and remains a diverse, uncentered movement expressing a divisive and sectarian spirit.

Gloss, textual: Used in text critical studies, a gloss signifies instances in which a scribal copyist or final editor of a text has inserted a word or phrase to elucidate an obscurity or make a theological point. An example is Genesis 10:14, where mention of Philistines has been added.

Glossolalia: Speaking in other tongues, or languages; an ecstatic spiritual state reported in the early church (Acts 2:1-13; 1 Cor. 12:10) and practiced in some Pentecostal and charismatic groups that believe the utterances to be of the Holy Spirit.

Gnosticism: A modern designation for a religious and philosophical view of the world that understands knowledge (*gnosis*) of reality to be attainable only by divine disclosure and which sees the goal of human existence as the liberation of the soul from its captive state in the material world. A Gnostic library discovered in Egypt in 1945 at Nag Hammadi contains accounts of creation and teachings of Jesus, which circulated from the second century until censored in the fourth.

Good Friday: The day commemorating Jesus Christ's death on the cross, probably April 3, C.E. 33. In the liturgical calendar of the Western church, the Friday before Easter.

Gospel: The English word derives from an Anglo-Saxon term meaning "God's story "(*godspel*). But the word enters the language of the Bible as a translation of the Greek *evangelion*, "good news." When the NT was written, the verb "to evangelize" or "preach the gospel" was an activity of public or private speaking, and the gospel was the content of what was uttered, not what was written down or read. The use of "gospel" in the sense of written documents (for example, Mathew, Mark, Luke and John) came much later in Justin's description of Sunday worship at Rome in 150 C.E.

Grace: God's freely given, unmerited gift of forgiveness and salvation.

Hanukkah: The eight-day Jewish festival of "dedication" that recalls the first fight for religious freedom in recorded history.

Hasidism: A mystical revivalist movement originating among Polish Jews in the eighteenth century. Underlying all Hasidic thought was the kabbalistic concept of the world as an emanation and reflection of "higher worlds." *Kavanah*, inner devotion, is central to Hasidic spirituality.

Hebrew Bible: The basic and most sacred collection of books of the Jewish people. In Hebrew the Bible is most commonly called TaNaKh—an acronym made up of the first letters of *Torah* ("Instruction," "Law"), *Nevi'im* ("Prophets"), and *Ketuvim* ("Writings"). Christians call the Hebrew Bible the Old Testament.

Heresy: Broadly, dissent from doctrine or belief upheld by an authoritative body or canon.

Hermeneutics: Derived from the Greek term *hermeneutikos*, it means interpretation or explanation and understanding of the meaning of a text. Applied before the nineteenth century mainly to interpretation of Jewish and Christian scriptures, hermeneutics has come to include methods for interpreting any text, subject, object, situation, or discipline (as in political hermeneutics).

Holy Spirit: In Christian theology the Holy Spirit is ranked within the Godhead as divine and, since the early creeds, worshiped as a member of the Holy Trinity. In Hebrew the term *rûah* is rendered by "spirit" or "wind," from a verb meaning "to blow or breathe." It is thus associated with the principle of life or "center of activity." The term occurs nearly four hundred times in the Hebrew Bible. Paul is the greatest NT exponent of the Christian life as "living in the Spirit" (Rom. 8:14-17; Gal. 4:6). The Spirit is the author of new life for the believer and the community, usually connected with the exaltation of the risen Lord and an initiatory rite of baptism.

Humanism: A cultural movement usually identified with the Renaissance revival (circa 1350-1600) of Greco-Roman-Hebraic antiquities. It represents a gradual shift from other-worldly to this-worldly concerns, symbolized in Protagoras' statement that the human is "the measure of all things."

Idolatry: Both in the Bible and in modern usage, this term ranges in meaning from the narrow sense of offering sacrifice and prayer to a material representation of deity ("an idol"), to the broad sense of treating as of ultimate importance some person, thing or concept other than God.

Incarnation: The most central but perhaps also the most complex of all Christian doctrines, it teaches that in Jesus Christ the second person of the Trinity assumed humanity, that he was and is fully human and fully God, and that this hypostatic union (as it is called) will never cease.

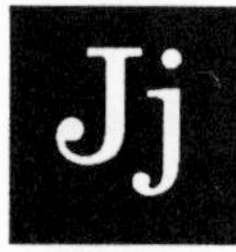

Judgment: A biblical teaching that all people are accountable for their moral actions, and that they will be summoned at a time of reckoning.

Justification: From the Latin *justificatio* to translate the Greek *dikaisosis,* used in the Pauline Epistles to signify right relationship with God and understood as an unearned gift.

Kabbala: The traditional name for mysticism in Judaism and for Jewish mystical teachings from the twelfth century C.E. through the middle ages.

Karma: From the Sanskrit word meaning "action," karma signifies that one's state and conditions are determined by behavior in previous lives.

Laity: From the Greek word *laos,* meaning "people," it refers to members of the church who are not clergy.

Liberalism: As a theological movement, a nineteenth century development that reached its zenith in the early twentieth century. Liberal Catholicism stems from French Revolutionary ideals and originally called for separation of church and state and freedom of religion, press and association. In Germany advocates sought to interpret dogma in more experiential and historical terms. Protestant Liberals share a suspicion of speculative theology, consider dogma secondary, cherish human rights and reason, endorse critical scholarship of the Bible and ecclesiatical tradition, and emphasize practical ethical imperatives of the Hebrew prophets and of Jesus.

Liberation Theology: Designates various Christian theologies concerned with social justice, freedom from oppression, God's liberating action in history, and empowerment of the oppressed rather than charity from oppressors. First articulated by Juan Luis Segundo and Gustavo Gutierrez, liberation theology addresses third world, black and feminist experiences of injustice.

Life Cycle: In psychology, aspects of the psyche that develop through the course of a lifetime in stages: infancy, childhood, adolescence, adulthood and maturity. Described by psychoanalyst Eric Erikson, the concept has been used to discuss moral development in the work of Carol Gilligan, and to analyze spiritual growth.

Litany: An ancient prayer form consisting of the presiding minister's invocation or petition and the worshipers' responses.

Liturgy: Spoken public worship by congregations.

Magi: From the Greek *magos,* referring to those trained in astrology and dream interpretation, originally members of the Persian priestly caste as early as 6 B.C.E. Matt. 2:1-16 tells of the magi whose observation of a star led them to Jerusalem the night Jesus was born.

Manna: Of uncertain origin, in Exod. 16:15 it is given a popular etymology *man hu,* meaning "what is it?" Manna was the miraculous food on which the Israelites were fed during their journey from Egypt into Canaan, according to the biblical history of the exodus.

Mantra: From the Sanskrit word meaning "instrument of thought," it is used in Hindu and Buddhist traditions to indicate verbal formulae, chants, hymns, or words recited to evoke spiritual force or to align oneself with a particular deity.

Meditation: Methodical reflection on external truths; a religious exercise thought to involve the mind, soul and body. Meditation plays a role in all religions, ancient and modern, in the form of discursive or mental prayer.

Merit: In Roman Catholic theology, the concept of a work or action that rightly deserves reward from God.

Millennialism: A belief system concerning the period of one thousand years in which the kingdom of God is to be ushered in by the Second Coming of Christ.

Miracle: A demonstration of the power of God, for which there is no scientific or natural explanation.

Mishnah: The oldest post-biblical collection of Jewish laws, compiled from 450 B.C.E. until about 200 C.E.

Modernism: Describes a variety of religious and theological movements, all of which have sought consciously to adapt Christianity to the modern world.

Moral Majority: A political coalition of conservative Protestants, Roman Catholics, Jews and Mormons banded together to exert influence on the U.S. government on behalf of various social, political and economic issues. The movement was founded by fundamentalist pastor Jerry Falwell in 1979.

Mysticism: Broadly, a form of religious experience that emphasizes immediate awareness of God and union with the divine, and implies commitment to a life process to that end.

Narrative Theology: A prominent discussion of theology as "story," which explores human nature portrayed in classic literature (including the modern novel) and treats of the Bible, myths, symbols, rites and images as elements of the story of God.

Natural Religion and Theology: Natural religion flourished among intellectuals of the seventeenth and eighteenth centuries and was understood as a distillation of revealed or positive religion. Its claim, based on the premises of natural theology, is that by the power of reason and observation, the human mind can attain elementary knowledge of God, of the soul's immortality and of morality. The physical universe, *i.e.*, creation is the locus of revealed knowledge.

Neo-Orthodoxy: A movement in Protestant theology that began in Switzerland after the outbreak of WWI, also referred to as "dialectical theology" or "the theology of crisis." It was the most influential and, in some respects, the most creative theological movement of the first half of this century. Protesting bourgeois liberal theology, Karl Barth initiated the movement with a call to base theological inquiry on biblical revelation and the meaning of being human.

New Age Movement: Broadly, a diverse, interreligious and optimistic set of unorthodox beliefs and practices popularized widely in the last decade. Adherents generally hold a blend of Eastern and Western spiritual teachings which include belief in some sacred scriptures, the reality of miracles, angels or guides, the immortality of the soul, reincarnation, animism, clairvoyance, astral projection, extraterrestrial life, astrology and the unity of body, mind and spirit. Many practice yoga or some form of meditation.

Nihilism: The doctrine of negation, or the assertion that there are no rational grounds for belief in moral or religious truth or values. Nihilism is often accompanied by radical expressions of personal freedom and is associated with the work of Friedrich Nietszche (1844-1900).

Omnipotence: From the Latin word meaning "all-powerful," and in classical Christian theology applied to God. The idea of God's omnipotence raises the question of evil and its origins in an all-powerful Creator.

Omnipresence: An attribute of God in classical Christian theology, the term is derived from the Latin word meaning "present everywhere." The idea implies the contradiction that evil exists in a world where God is everywhere.

Oral Tradition: The transmission of stories, teachings and illustrations of the biblical past told by word of mouth before becoming fixed in writing.

Orders and Ordination: In Roman Catholic theology, "orders," imply ordination, or the state of being consecrated and set apart for the Christian ministry. To be in orders or holy orders refers generally to the ranks of deacon, priest and bishop. Ordination is the sacrament (in Roman Catholic theology) of conferring such holy orders and in Protestantism, the ritual by which persons are set apart for the ministry of word and sacrament (or ordinances, in free churches). Protestant ordination is usually to one rank of ministry; that is, to the office of presbyter or pastor.

Original sin: The doctrine that throughout the history of the human race, human nature has been flawed. The doctrine's chief basis is the story of creation and the fall in the early chapters of Genesis, in which Adam and Eve pass on to the human race the consequences of choosing forbidden substance: a view Augustine (354-430) associated with pride and hereditary sin involving concupiscence.

Orthodoxy: From the Greek words *orthos* ("correct") and *doxa* ("opinion"), meaning the holding or practice of "right" belief; in contrast to heresy or heterodoxy, or the departing from established belief or doctrine.

Palm Sunday: The Sunday before Easter, celebrating the entry of Jesus into Jerusalem before his arrest, trial and crucifixion.

Panentheism: A form of theism or belief in the existence (or being) of God held by the philosophical theologian Paul Tillich (1886-1965) and process theologians associated with Alfred North Whitehead (1861-1947). Tillich held that everything exists in God, yet God is not the unity of all. Process thinkers recognize that God includes the world and that God changes as a result of experiencing the world. Process thought departs from the orthodox notion of God as immutable.

Pantheism: Religious and philosophical doctrine or belief that identifies the world with God and God with physical reality, thus stressing divine immanence and negating the idea of transcendence.

Parable: An extended metaphor that narrates a situation analogous to ordinary circumstance, told in such a way as to suggest the mystery or teaching of the metaphor. The genre is prevalent in the sayings of Jesus.

Paradise: In Jewish and Christian thought, the Persian loanword "paradise" is linked with the location of God's presence, where peace and absolute harmony prevail; conceived classically as a garden (Eden) of delight (cf. Gen. 2:8-14).

Parish: A territorial district served by a Roman Catholic Church, whose pastor oversees and conducts spiritual work with the laity. In Protestant usage it refers to the people within a territory who attend a specific church.

Paschal: Pertaining to Easter, the festival of the resurrection.

Passover: In the Hebrew Bible, the spring festival of freedom, celebrated by Jews to commemorate the Exodus of the Israelites from Egypt. Jesus observed Passover according to the Gospels.

Pastoral Epistles: The name designates the NT letters attributed to Paul and addressed to Timothy and Titus.

Pastoral Theology: The study of the practical work of the clergy, frequently called pastoral care or counseling and the practice of ministry.

Patristics: The study of writings of early Christian thinkers, proceedings of councils, ecclesiastical pronouncements, and related matters to about 600 C.E. Prominent patristic writers include Irenaeus, Tertullian, Origen, Athanasius and Augustine.

Patron Saint: In the Roman Catholic church, a saint venerated as a special protector of a specific city, profession, group, activity, nation or individual.

Penance: From the Latin *poenitentia,* meaning "to regret" and implying repentance for sins. Penance may be understood as personal, public, and in the Roman Catholic church, as canonical and sacramental.

Pentateuch: The first five books of the Hebrew Bible (Genesis, Exodus, Numbers, Deuteronomy and Leviticus), the so-called "five books of Moses" known in Judaism simply as Torah. Nineteenth and twentieth-century biblical scholars of form and source criticism have shown the Pentateuch was written by at least four anonymous editors or redactors known as J (Yahwist), E (Elohist), D (Deuteronomist) and P (Priestly).

Pentecost: The Feast of Weeks, the second of three festivals on which every male Jew was required to worship at Temple (Exod. 34:22-23; 2 Chron. 8:12-13). It means "fifty days" because the feast falls seven weeks after the opening of the harvest season (Lev. 23:15-16). For Christians the most important Pentecost festival took place after Jesus' resurrection. On that day the Holy Spirit came upon believers and gave them the power of xenoglossy, or the ability to speak and be understood in foreign languages (Acts 2:1-13). Pentecost in the Christian year is the fiftieth day after Easter.

Pentecostal Churches: A conservative evangelical grouping of several denominations that stresses the necessity of believers to receive the baptism of the Holy Spirit, an experience to occur subsequent to conversion.

Pharisees: Meaning "separated," a Jewish sect that emerged between 5 B.C.E. and 1 C.E., possibly as a result of the separatist teachings of Ezra after the return from Babylonian and Persian exile. Politically powerful scholars, the Pharisees codified what is called the Talmud (rabbinic interpretations of the Torah), and taught high regard for the elderly, conduct of reason, the immortality of the soul, the resurrection of the body, and freedom of will. They were confronted by Jesus (Matt. 15:3-9; Mark 7:6-8).

Pietism: A reaction against seventeenth century rationalism and Protestant scholasticism, pietism proposed a life of deep and personal experience of God. Its founder, Philipp Spener (1635-1705), promoted pietistic reform that influenced John Wesley (1703-91), founder of the Methodist movement.

Polytheism: Belief in and worship of many gods.

Predestination: The doctrine that God, from the beginning, has determined the ultimate destiny of every human being, either for salvation and eternal life, or not. Those predestined to salvation are said to be "elected," that is, "chosen" by God. The doctrine appears in the Hebrew Bible and the New Testament.

Principality: From the Greek *arché,* meaning "rule" or "dominion," one of the names in the New Testament given to angelic or demonic forces in Hellenistic cosmology, thought to control human destiny (cf. Rom. 8:38). In Titus 3:1 the term is used of earthy authorities in the Roman Empire.

Proof text: In biblical studies, an illegitimate use of scripture in which texts are isolated from their context and cited as probative evidence without regard for the situational meaning of the original authors; for example, "proof" creation took place during 4,004 B.C.E. on the basis of genealogies in Gen. 5. A secondary meaning refers to authorial use of scriptures to ground a claim or belief, such as Paul's references to the Hebrew Bible as prefigurations of the Messiah.

Prophet: In the Judeo-Christian tradition, a messenger and interpreter of God's will, some of whom were court counselors, such as Isaiah; others like John lived in the wilderness or in mountain caves. Prophets were regarded as clairvoyant "seers" and oracles.

Protestant Ethic: More fully, the Protestant work ethic, an attitude toward hard work and asceticism as virtues whose reward, a sign of divine favor, is accumulation of wealth. German sociologist Max Weber (1864-1920) coined the concept in *The Protestant Ethic and the Spirit of Capitalism* (1905).

Protestantism: The movement that developed out of religious and political events which attended attempts to reform the Roman Catholic Church. Protestantism grew out of teachings of the sixteenth century Reformation, when certain German princes and representatives signed the *Protestatio* document in 1529, supporting Martin Luther and disavowing supremacy of papal authority. Today the term Protestantism designates that segment of Christendom that is not allied with the churches of Eastern Orthodoxy or the Roman Catholic Church.

Providence: Derived from the Latin *providere,* "to foresee," providence means that God foresees and brings about future events.

Pseudepigrapha: Sacred Jewish writings from a few centuries before and after Christ that are not included in the Bible, Apocrypha, or rabbinic literature.

Purgatory: In Roman Catholic doctrine, the state in which the souls of the dead suffer, through the pain of longing to see the beatific vision of God, until they are purged of unforgiven venial sins, or the punishment by God for forgiven mortal sins so that souls may enter heaven.

Puritans: Originally, those within the Church of England in the 1560s who opposed the Elizabethan Settlement and wished to further purify the church of all "popish" forms, especially vestments, and to adhere strictly to the theology of Calvisim. The Puritans also represented the rising gentry and market capitalism. Puritans hailed the Bible as authority, although in Oxford by the seventeenth century, championed the new physical sciences of the Enlightenment. For church membership they required a personal conversion experience and in principle advocated freedom of conscience.

Q (Quelle): Symbolizes the written or oral source used by the authors of Matthew, Mark and Luke in the composition of their gospels. Known as the "second source" (the Gospel of Mark being the first and earliest of NT writings), Q may have been a handbook recording oral traditions about Jesus that originally circulated in his language, Aramaic, and possibly in Greek as well.

Quietism: The term used for a movement in seventeenth century Roman Catholicism; a form of spirituality that called for extreme passivity of the soul and the suppression of all human effort, including good works and ascetical activity. Quietism was condemned as a heresy in 1687.

Qur'an: From the Arabic word for "recited," Qur'an is the sacred scripture of Islam (sometimes spelled Koran).

Rabbi: Jewish teacher, preacher and spiritual leader. The office of rabbi was created in the middle ages, when the rabbi was the recognized leader of the community and the official Jewish legal authority.

Rastafari Movement: A politico-religious movement among Jamaican blacks, begun in 1930. Their belief is that blacks are the true heirs of biblical Israel and that Ras (Prince) Tafari, crowned as Emperor Haile Selassie of Ethiopia in the year of the movement's founding, would be their messiah.

Rationalism: A term used for a variety of movements in Western philosophy and theology. The word signifies that reason rather than experience, tradition, or authority is the final arbiter in matters of knowledge and truth. Rationalism is often contrasted with empiricism, the latter basing knowledge on experience and observation rather than the innate ideas or *a priori* categories of the mind.

Redemption: Basically meaning "deliverance," redemption signifies in the Hebrew Bible liberation from slavery or captivity, often by payment of a ransom or an act of clemency. In the New Testament, redemption describes the release from slavery to sin through God in Christ.

Reformation, Protestant: The sixteenth century ecclesiastical separations from Roman Catholicism initiated by Martin Luther's discovery of justification or righteousness by faith alone, and his reliance on scriptures as an authority greater than that of the Pope in Rome. His Ninety-five Theses nailed to a Wittenberg church door in 1517 protested the selling of indulgences to cancel out sins, along with abuses that had corrupted the Catholic Church. Luther's theological and practical differences with the Church prompted political, economic, social and intellectual change that altered the course of Western civilization.

Regeneration: Literally "bath of rebirth" or Christian baptism, the term signifies the new order of existence, both cosmic and personal, promised in Jesus Christ.

Reincarnation: A belief that the soul, spirit, or essential self passes into another physical body after death, perhaps after a time in an intermediate state. Reincarnation is most central to Hinduism and Buddhism; in the West, Plato taught reincarnation as the transmigration of the soul.

Repentance: From the Greek *metanoia,* meaning "change of mind," repentance concerns transformation brought about by conversion and turning away from evil.

Resurrection of Jesus: That God raised Jesus from the dead is the central and distinctive claim of the early church. Throughout the New Testament, witnesses such as Mary and Paul report appearances of the risen Jesus after his crucifixion. The NT community shared the belief that the resurrection of Jesus is both the instrument and demonstration of his role as the one through whom God's kingdom is established on earth.

Revivalism: As a modern phenomenon, the movement that grew out of the Puritan emphasis on conversion as a personal commitment and on the necessity of such a conversion for church membership. Revivals are the Protestant religious corollary of "awakenings" or periods of national and cultural crisis in beliefs and values. In America, Puritanism and the so-called Great Awakenings from the eighteenth to twentieth centuries exemplify revivalism identified with Jonathan Edwards, Cotton Mather, Dwight Moody and Billy Graham.

Right to Life Movement: A descriptive term arising during the anti-abortion struggle in the U.S., especially after the Supreme Court legalized abortion (during the first two trimesters of pregnancy) on January 22, 1973. The movement originated among Roman Catholics.

Rosh Hashanah: The Jewish New Year, observed with prayer, contemplation and self examination.

Rule of Faith: A summary of the Christian faith as handed down from the apostles through the bishops, used primarily as a standard in catechetical instruction and as a guide for the interpretation of scripture in preaching.

Sacerdotal: Having to do with sacred things, with the divine liturgy and the duties of a priest.

Sacrament: A significant rite or action that makes present or effective the sacred or holy. Sacraments are found in all religions in which the divine or supernatural is made present through the natural. Augustine defined a sacrament as a "visible sign of an invisible reality." Sacramental actions include baptisms and purification rites, common sacred meals (in the Christian tradition, the eucharist), and rites of initiation and confirmation.

Sadducees: An aristocratic Jewish sect of high priestly families, lesser priests and nobility who participated in the rule of the Jewish homeland from the years following the Maccabean wars of independence to the revolt against Rome, about 160 B.C.E. to 70 C.E. The Sadducees rejected belief in bodily resurrection and rewards of the world to come (Mark 12:18-27; Acts 23:6-8).

Saints, Veneration of: The practice began in the early Christian church with the belief that martyrs gained immediate entry into heaven and that their intercession with God was particularly effective.

Salvation: A key biblical term for several aspects of the divine enterprise in restoring humankind to God and of the human response to that initiative. The three major emphases of the word are: (1) to be set free from the peril of physical or spiritual dangers; (2) to be restored to health and wholeness (Heb. *shalom;* the NT equivalent is "peace" with God, one's neighbor or oneself); (3) to be rescued from death in the face of mortal peril or separation from God through sin.

Samadhi: From the Sanskrit for "total collectedness," the Hindu word for the highest state of consciousness.

Sanctification: In biblical theology and spirituality, the process of growth in personal sanctity or holiness, accomplished by God's freely given grace as a stage of salvation which follows justification.

Satori: A Japanese word used in Zen to indicate enlightenment, meaning literally "surprise."

Scholasticism: The theological and philosophical movement dominant in Europe from about the seventh century until the emergence of modern philosophy in the sixteenth century, and which continues to be esteemed in the Roman Catholic Church today. Scholastics held that faith and reason are one, and drew on the revealed truths of Christian thought and on the resources of classical philosophy; especially Aristotle. Prominent scholastic thinkers include Anselm, Abelard, Aquinas and Ockham.

Scopes Trial: Famed legal case in 1925 involving the teaching of evolution in a public school and against Tennessee law. John T. Scopes, a biology teacher, was found guilty and fined for presenting a "theory that denies the story of Divine Creation."

Secularism: From the Latin *saeculum,* referring to time. The "temporal" differs with the "eternal" and by implication, the worldly with the religious. Secularism denotes value of human achievement and of social, political and cultural experience and institutions.

Separatism: The tendency for a religious group to separate itself from a mother group in order to purify the group's life or restore its doctrine to a more pristine form. Separatists include early American Puritans and early Baptists and Congregationalists.

Septuagint: The name of the earliest Greek translation of the Hebrew Bible, denoted by LXX.

Sermon on the Mount: The collection of teachings that Jesus is reported in Matt. 5-7 to have delivered to the crowds that were following him.

Seven Gifts of the Holy Spirit: In Paul's Epistle to the Romans (Rom. 12:6-8), prophecy, service, teaching, exhortation, liberality, enthusiasm, and mercy with cheerfulness.

Seven Virtues: According to Roman Catholic moral theology, the four cardinal virtues prudence, justice, fortitude and temperance, plus the three theological virtues faith, hope and charity (that is, love). A virtue is a lasting disposition of the soul.

Shalom: Popularly translated from the Hebrew as "peace" and used in greeting or taking leave of someone.

Shi'ite: The "separate party" of Islam, a collection of diverse groups and movements that arose in opposition to the first three caliphs. The Shi'ites believe that Ali, the fourth caliph, was the mandated successor to Muhammad the prophet.

Shroud of Turin: An ancient linen cloth imprinted with the image of a man that was thought to be Jesus. The shroud, in which Joseph of Arimathea and Nicodemus are said to have wrapped the body of Jesus, is in the Cathedral in Turin, Italy.

Sinaiticus, Codex: Fourth century C.E. manuscript discovered in 1844 in a monastery on Mount Sinai; the only early Greek manuscript containing the entire New Testament.

Situation Ethics: A concept coined by Joseph Fletcher in 1959 to propose a situational method—that is, pragmatic, relativistic and personal—for making moral decisions based on love.

Skepticism: Denotes a general attitude of doubt and, secondarily, a philosophical tradition originating in ancient Greece that questions the possibility of authentic knowledge.

Social Darwinism: A term for the use of evolutionary ideas, drawn from the writings of Charles Darwin and Herbert Spencer and applied to ethics, social theory and history.

Social Gospel: The general teaching of the late nineteenth and early twentieth centuries optimists who sought to relate the Christian gospel to the American industrial social environment; attributed to Walter Rauschenbusch (1861-1918).

Soteriology: The doctrine of salvation or redemption, which explains in varied ways how humans are reconciled to God.

Spiritualism: A philosophical doctrine called idealism, which holds only spirit or mind is real. Popularly, reference to beliefs and practices of those who believe it is possible to communicate with the dead.

Stations of the Cross: Fourteen symbols representing incidents in Christ's walk from his condemnation by Pilate to the cross.

Synoptic Gospels: The first three canonical gospels, traditionally ascribed to Mathew, Mark and Luke, all of which share a generally common presentation of the events of Jesus' life, death and resurrection.

Systematic Theology: The attempt to present the entire body of Christian beliefs as a system of truth in which each doctrine is related to every other doctrine. Its supposition is that there is one truth, of God in Jesus Christ.

T'ai Chi: From the Chinese term for "Great Ultimate," it represents the cosmic unity through which the Tao or universal way expresses itself. Also, an ancient Chinese meditative dance now taught in America.

Talmud: A vast and varied work interpreting Jewish legal and moral responsibilities as set forth in the Bible and discussed by rabbis and scholars over a period of about seven hundred years, circa 200 B.C.E.—500 C.E. The Talmud consists of the Mishnah, a collection of Jewish law and the Gemara, or commentary on the Mishnah.

Taoism: From the Chinese *Tao* (pronounced dow), meaning "way," a religious and philosophical tradition that stresses immortality and the greatest good as harmonious living following the *Tao*, best discerned in nature and human relationships.

Teleology: The idea of a purposive structure within an organism and the theory that ends are inherent in the nature of things. In the twentieth century, teleology concerns the problems of structure and function and differs from Darwinism or a view of life as a process evolving by natural selection. For example, Christian teleology affirms that life is directed by God toward completion of a divine plan.

Theism: The basic religious doctrine of Christians, Jews and Muslims that God exists.

Tithe: From ancient times, the tenth part of a person's income and/or property devoted to religious use as an offering, or to political use as a tax or tribute.

Torah: Scroll of the law and teaching, read in the synagogue on the Jewish Sabbath, Mondays and Thursdays, and on Jewish holy days. In rabbinic literature "Torah" also refers to the Pentateuch as distinct from the two other sections of the Hebrew Bible—the Prophets and theWritings—and indeed to all the teachings of Judaism, its laws, doctrines, ethics, philosophy, customs and ceremonies.

Transcendence: From the Latin *trans scandere,* to "climb over." Contrasted with immanence, transcendence attributed to God classically describes an unmoved mover or being external to the universe.

Transcendentalism: An American contribution to philosophy and theology, an outgrowth of German idealism and English romanticism expressed in Ralph Waldo Emerson's work during the nineteenth century. Transcendentalists believed the universe was centered in one mind and oversoul active in nature.

Transcendental Meditation: A technique from the Hindu tradition brought to the West by Mahareshi Mahesh Yogi. It is a process of turning inward to transcend thought and expand consciousness.

Trinity: Meaning literally "threeness," this term is used of the Christian doctrine that God is three persons in one substance or one substance in three persons: Father, Son and Holy Ghost.

Unification Church: A worldwide movement founded by the Reverend Sun Myung Moon in Korea in 1954, whose members are known informally as "Moonies." Charges of recruiting by mind control of some 35,000 young Americans by the 1980s have relegated the church to the status of a cult.

United Bible Societies: A world fellowship of sixty-four national Bible societies, founded in 1946. The UBS organizes training institutes and publishes technical helps for translators, produces and distributes Bibles, and aids millions of new literates in Bible reading.

Universalism: The doctrine that in the end all souls will be saved by God's grace. It has been revived by liberal theologians who have found the idea of eternal punishment repellent. Neo-orthodox theologian Karl Barth has taught a form of universalism, holding the entire human race has been elected in Jesus Christ.

Utilitarianism: The theory that right action is one that brings happiness or the best possible good for the greatest number, and that no action in itself is morally right or wrong but becomes so when the consequences are known.

Values relativism: Affirms that human goals and rules of conduct depend upon the cultural context, and that the goodness and rightness of actions are relative to particular circumstances.

Vatican: The residence of the pope, head of the Roman Catholic Church, located in the city of the Vatican, an autonomous state on Vatican hill in Rome. The palace of the Vatican is the international headquarters of the R.C. Church.

Vatican Councils: Two important church-wide councils held by the Roman Catholic Church, in 1869-70 and in 1962-65. Vatican I was the twentieth ecumenical council and was adjourned in 1870 when the Italian army captured Rome from papal forces. It declared papal infallibility a part of Christian doctrine. At Vatican II five major issues were debated: the liturgy, sources of revelation, the communications media, church unity, and the nature and structure of the church. As a result most aspects of ecclesiology and Roman theology were modernized.

Vedas: The ancient sacred scriptures of Hinduism preserved as sacred songs and chants of an oral tradition written comparatively recently, together with ritual and philosophical commentary.

Vespers: The evening service in Roman Catholic churches of the Latin rite, as well as in monastic, cathedral and collegiate churches. In Protestant churches it is the normal evening service.

Virgin Birth: The Gospels of Mathew and Luke agree in reporting that Mary conceived Jesus by the Holy Spirit and without intercourse (Matt. 1:18-21; Luke 1:26-38). In both accounts Joseph and Mary were betrothed, but had not had sexual relations at the time Jesus was born.

Vulgate: The Latin translation of the Bible by Jerome, a fourth century scholar.

Way, The: An international religious movement founded by Victor Paul Wierwille (1917-85), a former evangelical and reformed minister and charismatic personality who attracted youth of the Jesus People era.

Will of God: A prevalent teaching in Middle and Far Eastern religions, but less evident in the Western world, where the belief in freedom of the will counterbalances deterministic world views associated with the absolute sovereignty of God. Both Hebrew Bible and New Testament stress the will of God in the context of human choice to follow and do it.

Witness: In the Hebrew Bible, the equivalent of "testimony" and a rudiment of the legal system as evidence for an event such a the covenant and presence of Yahweh. In the New Testament, Paul appeals to his honesty as an apostle to witness especially to the resurrection of Jesus Christ. In Johannine literature, witness is synonymous with "preaching the gospel."

Word, The: A title for the preincarnate Lord who became human, in Johannine theology. Another term is *logos,* Greek for "word." In Greek philosophy, with which John was acquainted, the word was regarded as a divine principle underlying the cosmos. The Hebrew Bible gives the word a personalized rendering as an attribute of God active in creation or as a personification of God in revelation, chiefly through the Law, the Torah, wisdom, or the Prophets.

World Council of Churches: First convened in Amsterdam in 1948, the formal organization to coordinate an authoritative body to be a mouthpiece to government and to create church unity across Christendom—hence the locus of the ecumenical movement.

Yaweh: The personal name for the Israelite national Deity, usually translated "the Lord." Reproduced in ancient Hebrew texts as the Tetragrammaton YHWH, a name later pronounced only on special occasions by the high priest, its meaning is uncertain; although Exod. 3:14 suggests it may have been connected with the verb "to be."

Yoga: Literally "discipline," a term that includes a variety of beliefs and practices in Hinduism. In the U.S. the feature best known is a set of physical exercises, with emphasis on proper posture and disciplined breathing. Hindu practitioners understand yoga to designate three ways of conducting the religious life: devotion to deity, doing one's duty without attachment to the results of action, and gaining true knowledge.

Zen: A form of Mahayana Buddhism that arose in China circa 500 C.E. and spread to Korea and Japan. While other Buddhist schools have stressed ultimate reality, Zen has placed emphasis on the mind and Nirvana as the original Buddha mind or nature.

Zionism: The belief in the restoration of the Jewish people to Zion, a poetic name for Jerusalem and the land of Israel. Political Zionism aimed to create for the Jewish people a home in Palestine secured by public law: the State of Israel established in 1948. Cultural Zionism saw Palestine as a "spiritual center" from which the spirit of the Jewish people outside the promised land would be revived. Religious Zionism projected a concept of religious nationalism asserting "the thought-image of Jewish nationality lay in the unity of the Jewish people with its Torah and its faith."

Note: Most definitions have been adapted with permission from *The Dictionary of Bible and Religion*, William H. Gentz, General Editor (Nashville: Abingdon Press), 1986.

X. Methodology

Design of the Samples

For Personal Surveys:
The design of the sample for personal (face-to-face) surveys is that of a replicated area probability sample down to the block level in the case of urban areas and to segments of townships in the case of rural areas.

After stratifying the nation geographically and by size of community according to information derived from the most recent census, over 350 different sampling locations are selected on a mathematically random basis from within cities, towns and counties that have in turn been selected on a mathematically random basis.

The interviewers are given no leeway in selecting the areas in which they are to conduct their interviews. Each interviewer is given a map on which a specific starting point is marked, and is instructed to contact households according to a predetermined travel pattern. At each occupied dwelling unit, the interviewer selects respondents by following a systematic procedure. This procedure is repeated until the assigned number of interviews has been completed.

For Telephone Surveys:
The national Gallup telephone samples are based on the area probability sample used for personal surveys.

In each of the sampling locations selected (as described above), a set of telephone exchanges that falls within the geographic boundaries of the sampling location is first identified. Listed telephone numbers in these exchanges are selected randomly and used as "seed numbers" for randomly generating telephone numbers. The result of this procedure is a sample of listed and unlisted telephone numbers assigned to households within telephone exchanges serving our sampling locations. The final sample of numbers thus reflects the stratification and selection of sampling locations that provide confidence in the representativeness of our area probability sample.

After the survey data have been collected and processed, each respondent is assigned a weight so that the demographic characteristics of the total weighted sample of respondents matches the latest estimates of the demographic characteristics of the appropriate adult population available from the U.S. Census Bureau. Telephone surveys are weighted to match the characteristics of the adult population living in households, with access to a telephone. The weighting of personal interview data includes a factor to improve the representation of the kinds of people who are less likely to be found at home.

The procedures described above are designed to produce samples approximating the adult civilian population (18 and older) living in private households (that is, excluding those in prisons, hospitals, hotels, religious and education institutions and those living on reservations or military bases) — and in the case of telephone surveys, households with access to a telephone. Survey percentages may be applied to census estimates of the size of these populations to project percentages into numbers of people. The manner in which the sample is drawn also produces a sample which approximates the distribution of private households in the United States; therefore, survey results can also be projected to numbers of households.

Sampling Tolerances

In interpretating survey results, it should be borne in mind that all sample survey are subject to sampling error, that is, the extent to which the results may differ from those that would be obtained if the whole population surveyed had been interviewed. The size of such sampling errors depends largely on the number of interviews.

The *Gallup Poll Accuracy Record* below may be used in estimating sampling error. The computed allowances have taken into account the effect of the sample design upon sampling error. They may be interpreted as indicating the range (plus or minus the figure shown) within which the results of repeated samplings in the same time period could be expected to vary, 95 percent of the time, assuming the same sampling procedure, the same interviewers, and the same questionnaire were used.

Table A below shows the allowances that should be made for the sampling error of a percentage.

The table should be used as follows: Say a reported percentage is 33 for a group which includes 1500 respondents. Go to the row labeled "percentages near 30" and then to the column headed "1500." The number at this point is 3, which means that the 33 percent obtained in the sample is subject to a sampling error of plus or minus 3 points. Another way of saying it is that very probably (95 times out of 100) the average of repeated samplings would be somewhere between 30 and 36, with the most likely figure the 33 obtained.

In comparing survey results in two sub-samples, such as men and women, the question arises as to how large a difference between them there must be before one can be reasonably sure that it reflects a real difference. In *Tables B* and *C* below, the number of points which must be allowed for in such comparisons is indicated.

For percentages near 20 or 80, use *Table B*, for those near 50, *Table C*. For percentages in between, the error factor is between that shown in the two tables.

Here is an example of how the tables should be used: Say 50% of men and 40% of women respond the same way to a question, a difference of 10 percentage points. Can it be said with any assurance that the 10 point difference reflects a real difference between the men and women on the question? Let us suppose that the sample contains 750 men and 750 women.

Because the percentages are near 50, consult *Table C*. Since the two sample are about 750 persons each, look for the place in the table where the column and row labeled "750" converge. The number seven appears there. This means the allowance for error should be seven points, and the conclusion that the percentage among men is somewhere between 3 and 17 points higher than the percentage among women would be wrong only about 5% of the time. In other words, there is a considerable likelihood that a difference exists in the direction observed and that it amounts to at least 3 percentage points.

If, in another case, 22% of male respondents answer a question in a particular way, compared to 24% of female respondents, consult *Table B* because these percentages are near 20. The column and row labeled "750" converge on the number five. Obviously then, the 2 point difference is inconclusive.

Table A
Allowance for Sampling Error of a Percentage
In Percentage Points
(at 95 in 100 confidence level*)

	Size of Sample						
	1500	1000	750	600	400	200	100
Percentages near 10	2	2	3	3	3	5	8
Percentages near 20	3	3	4	4	5	7	10
Percentages near 30	3	4	4	5	6	8	12
Percentages near 40	3	4	5	5	6	9	12
Percentages near 50	3	4	5	5	6	9	13
Percentages near 60	3	4	5	5	6	9	12
Percentages near 70	3	4	4	5	6	8	12
Percentages near 80	3	3	4	4	5	7	10
Percentages near 90	2	2	3	3	4	5	8

Table B
Allowance for Sampling Error of the Difference
In Percentage Points
(at 95 in 100 confidence level*)

Percentages near 20 or percentages near 80

Size of the Sample	750	600	400	200
750	5			
600	6	6		
400	6	7	7	
200	8	8	9	10

Table C
Percentages near 50

Size of the Sample				
750	7			
600	7	7		
400	8	8	9	
200	10	10	11	13

*The chances are 95 in 100 that the sampling error is not larger than the figures shown.

Gallup Poll Accuracy Record

Year	Gallup Final Survey		Election Results		Deviation
1988	56.0%	Bush	53.9%	Bush	– 2.1
1984	59.0	Reagan	59.2	Reagan	– 0.2
1982	55.0	Democratic	56.1	Democratic	– 1.1
1980	47.0	Reagan	50.8	Reagan	– 3.8
1978	55.0	Democratic	54.6	Democratic	+ 0.4
1976	48.0	Carter	50.0	Carter	– 2.0
1974	60.0	Democratic	58.9	Democratic	+ 1.1
1972	62.0	Nixon	61.8	Nixon	+ 0.2
1970	53.0	Democratic	54.3	Democratic	– 1.3
1968	43.0	Nixon	43.5	Nixon	– 0.5
1966	52.5	Democratic	51.9	Democratic	+ 0.6
1964	64.0	Johnson	61.3	Johnson	+ 2.7
1962	55.5	Democratic	52.7	Democratic	+ 2.8
1960	51.0	Kennedy	50.1	Kennedy	+ 0.9
1958	57.0	Democratic	56.5	Democratic	+ 0.5
1956	59.5	Eisenhower	57.8	Eisenhower	+ 1.7
1954	51.5	Democratic	52.7	Democratic	– 1.2
1952	51.0	Eisenhower	55.4	Eisenhower	– 4.4
1950	51.0	Democratic	50.3	Democratic	+ 0.7
1948	44.5	Truman	49.9	Truman	– 5.4
1946	58.0	Republican	54.3	Republican	+ 3.7
1944	51.5	Roosevelt	53.3	Roosevelt	– 1.8
1942	52.0	Democratic	48.0	Democratic	+ 4.0
1940	52.0	Roosevelt	55.0	Roosevelt	– 3.0
1938	54.0	Democratic	50.8	Democratic	+ 3.2
1936	55.7	Roosevelt	62.5	Roosevelt	– 6.8

Average deviation for 26 national elections: *2.2 percentage points*

Average deviation for 19 national elections since 1950, inclusive: *1.5 percentage points*

Trends in Deviation

Elections	Average Error
1936-1950	3.6
1952-1960	1.7
1962-1970	1.6
1972-1988	1.4